DATE DUE

People  You

JUL. 14.1997			
OCT. 24.1997			
NOV. 09.1998			
NOV. 23.1998			
MAY 03.1999			
GAYLORD			

To all of the people
who have worked tirelessly
for the cause of disability rights
in the United States

People with Disabilities Explain It All For You

Your Guide to the Public Accommodations Requirements of the Americans With Disabilities Act

edited by
Mary Johnson
& the Editors of *The Disability Rag*

The Advocado Press

CONTENTS

Foreword

The federal Americans with Disabilities Act, passed in 1990, promises to be the most far-reaching act of civil-rights legislation ever enacted. Every business or group doing business with the public is affected by this law. Discrimination against people with disabilities is forbidden both in employment and in public accommodations. And by "public accommodations" lawmakers meant practically every place open to the public. After January 26, 1992, all sorts of places, from laundromats to accountants' offices to groceries to theaters, will be violating the law if they refuse to accommodate someone with a disability.

To help those of you who run such places was our intention in putting together this book, *People With Disabilities Explain It All For You*. We designed it as an easy-to-read how-to guide for people who operate public accommodations. We believe it can assist anyone who wants to learn about opening their services to everyone.

This book is not a legal guide; it's not meant to substitute for legal advice.

Nor could we hope to explain everything about access and design that a contractor needs to know in renovating or building a facility with access in mind. What we have tried to do is give you some principles and a way to understand what it is you're supposed to do, with enough examples to help you to find your way. Throughout the book, we urge you to take advantage of the wealth of advice and material available to help you. It's a point we can't stress too much.

This book is not a guide to the employment provisions of Title I of the Act; it is only a guide to the law's Title III. But even though this book isn't about disabled people joining your workforce, it's not too soon to think about the possibility. We think this book will help you start that thinking process.

We wish all of you the best of luck in opening your places to those of us with disabilities. After all, it's the law. And, as you'll learn throughout this book, we believe it can be an easy and ultimately financially rewarding process.

Introduction
Who We Are
and What We Want From You

Every one of us knows someone who has a disability. But we usually don't think of it that way.

Do you have an uncle who had a stroke and is partially paralyzed?

Has your father lost his hearing as he's gotten older?

What about that buddy of yours who lost his leg in Vietnam and now has an artificial leg?

Or your cousin's little girl, born with Down Syndrome? Or your computer salesman, whose wife has multiple sclerosis? Your neighbor's son was in a car accident; he had a brain injury. He looks OK now, but he can't remember things very well and — well, he doesn't seem "right" all the time. And he has trouble walking.

All these people have trouble of one sort or another as they try to live their lives. We may not think of them as "disabled" or "handicapped," though. Most of us figure that if our mind or our body has something wrong with it, there are just things we can't do anymore. We can't drive cars, for instance; can't go out as much; certainly can't hold down a job. If our eyes go, we can't expect to read books or magazines anymore, or the daily paper, for that matter. That's just how it goes, we think.

But that thinking has been changing in America. Since the early 1970s, an increasing number of people who had polio, people who survived the Korean and Vietnam Wars with injuries (some of them extremely severe, paralyzing them almost totally) began to realize that there was no reason they could not continue to live their lives and try to contribute to society. Technology was making that possible. Increasingly sophisticated medical techniques were allowing people with severe disabilities to live. Newer wheelchairs, prostheses like artifical legs and arms were giving people more ability to get around, even though they had sustained severe injuries or survived terrible diseases.

Today, that technology is expanding. With the rapid computerization of modern everyday America, things undreamed of (or incredibly expensive) have become commonplace and downright cheap — things that have a side effect of making life easier for people who have specific disabilities. Consider, for example, talking watches, calculators and voice-input modules on everyday personal business computers. These now-everyday devices have made a world of difference to people who have lost their sight. Today it doesn't seem unusual to hear someone's watch "tell" the time in a crowded sales meeting. But years ago, before such devices were common, someone using one would have been considered "special." If he had one because he was very rich and could afford a new, cutting-edge "toy," he'd be admired. But if he were blind and were using it because he couldn't "read" an ordinary watch, he'd be pitied.

Technology has lessened the gap between people without disabilities and people with them. A man in a motorized wheelchair is no more "handicapped" than a walking man in going through an automatic door or tooling down the wide corridors of a mall, window shopping. A woman who's lost her hearing is no more "handicapped" than someone with full hearing when she's reading the newspaper or entering data on a computer.

But even with the many changes that have occured in recent years, many people who have no hearing, no vision or who can't walk, who are paralyzed, still find themselves shut out of much of what most of us take for granted. Even today's best technology has not closed the gap between people who can go into a sales meeting and deliver a rousing report without any assistance and the young executive in the wheelchair who must wait, first, for someone to open the door to the meeting room; wait for someone to remove the chairs and ask people to get out of the way so he can get up to the conference table, have someone open his briefcase and get out his reports.

A computer expert can come to your company to give a training, but if he happens to be blind, even though he's brought his notes in braille (which he printed out earlier in the day back at his office on the braille printer output from his computer workstation) he's apt to be thought of as "less competent" — because he's blind.

Once that the technology existed to make someone who was blind perform as capably as a sighted person, many blind people hoped that they would no longer be considered inferior when they applied for a job. But that didn't happen. One man, a Harvard graduate, was turned down at over 100 firms, he told Senate Committee members a few years ago, simply because he was blind. How did he know? His potential employers told him, flat out. The problem wasn't his grades, which were fine. The problem was simply that they didn't want a blind person working there. They didn't think — despite evidence to the contrary — that he could do the job.

This man's story has been experienced over and over by countless blind men and women in America. It has also been experienced by people with other sorts of disabiliies as well — people who are deaf, or who use wheelchairs, or who have something that seems "weird," like cerebral palsy or epilepsy, or who have a history of having been in a mental institution of one sort or another.

Our efforts to make life better

As long ago as the 1930s, people who had various kinds of disabilities (like polio, which President Franklin D. Roosevelt had) were banding together to find ways to make their lives better. Some worked for cures. But most of those who worked for cures were the parents of the people who had the disabilities. The people who had the disabilities themselves worked instead to better their lives here and now, whether there was any cure or not.

The National Federation of the Blind was one such group, which early on modeled itself on the labor movement in its effort to get better conditions for blind people and to insist, from its founding, that most of the problems blind people faced lay not in their blindness but in society's attitudes toward them. With braille (the raised-dot printing), with training in how to use a white cane to determine where they were walking, blind people claimed they were fully capable human beings — if only society would give them a chance. They also insisted that the focus on the great "courage" of someone like Helen Keller only showed how little sighted people understood of blind people, who were not "courageous" so much as determined to live an ordinary life despite the obstacles society, not blindness, threw up at every turn.

The Federation was one group. There were groups deaf people

formed, too, like the National Association of the Deaf. There were groups like the Congress of the Physically Handicapped. The Paralyzed Veterans of America is another such group. These groups worked so that people who had disabilities could partake of the American Dream without waiting to be "cured." Many such groups formed, some small, some large. Most focused only on a particular kind of physical disability. In the 1960s, however, people who had been working within these groups began to recognize that the problems they faced seemed to have a common pattern: whether blind, or deaf, or paralyzed from polio or a spinal cord injury, each person who had a disability was being told they were "less than." That they were incapable. That they couldn't work. That they couldn't be allowed into restaurants. That they had to use special transportation, not the regular buses and subways. That they had to go to special schools or receive home instruction — that they couldn't go to regular schools.

Though many of these "restrictions" weren't intentionally discriminatory, and certainly not malicious, they had the same effect as discriminatory treatment has had on other groups: it kept them out of society; it kept them poor; it kept them unemployed, drawing on welfare even though they would rather be working. This fact became clearer and clearer to those who worked to better their lives as disabled people.

The 1970s and 1980s saw a great amount of activity in passing laws both on the state level and the national level to try to help the people our society back then labelled "handicapped" enter the mainstream of American life. Many of the laws on the state level were aimed at getting rid of "architectural barriers" in public buildings such as steps, narrow doors, restrooms that no one in a wheelchair could use. States passed laws allowing blind people to have their guide dogs accompany them into places dogs weren't ordinarily allowed, such as restaurants. Some states where deaf people had strong organizations, such as California, passed laws requiring a relay phone service between deaf people who used "telephone devices for the deaf," or TDDS, and regular voice phones.

In 1973, a federal law called the Rehabilitation Act was passed. It was a fairly routine piece of federal legislation; there had been

Rehabilitation Acts before and they mostly served to provide money to states to train disabled people to get jobs. This time, however, congressional staffers, aware of the discrimination that disability groups were constantly pointing out, added a Title V to the Act which contained for the first time a "non-discrimination" requirement: federal programs, businesses receiving federal contracts, and programs getting public money could not discriminate against "handicapped" people in terms of offering goods or services.

Section 503 (for federal contractors) and Section 504 (for programs receiving federal dollars) of the Rehabilitation Act have been on the books for nearly two decades. Still, relatively few people know about the law. Its enforcement has been spotty. Even people whom it could help, like your Uncle Joe who had a stroke and who would have liked to have gone out more, didn't know about the law or how to use it.

Because of this Rehabilitation Act, however (as well as state laws requiring access), many buildings have had ramps installed and grab bars added to restrooms. Still, many people who had various kinds of disabilities did not come out and participate in society.

Why we need the Americans with Disabilities Act

Why not? That was the big question asked by many disabled people who were active in working on behalf of their peers. The answer: Neither the federal law nor the state laws *encompassed enough*. Their effect was spotty, at best. And that was a bigger problem than it might appear.

To illustrate the point, consider this story: A man who uses a motorized wheelchair, who is partially paralyzed from having had polio as a child, wants to go shopping. We'll call our mythical shopper "Bill."

Bill has money; that's not the problem. The problem is getting to the shop — and getting in.

Bill's city has a law (Bill's state has a law about this, too, as do most states) which requires that curb corners have ramps put into them. But the law's enforcement has been lax. Though there is a curb "cut" at the end of the man's block, there's no corresponding one across the street. And he has to get to the other side to get a bus.

This man is lucky, though. He lives in a city — Seattle — which has wheelchair lifts on most of its buses. Though the Rehabilitation Act required buses to be accessible, the transit industry fought that requirement for years, preferring to "serve" people like Bill with special van services. The problem with these services, from Bill's viewpoint (and yours too, if you'd been in Bill's shoes), is that, unlike a regular bus or subway or commuter train service, these vans had to be scheduled in advance — *anywhere from 24 hours to a week in advance!* As anyone knows who's had to run down to the electronics store to replace a broken cable on a computer when a big job is due, you can't always schedule when you need to run out and buy something. Though many disabled people argued and argued, in court and in the streets, that these "special van services" were unequal (for this, if no other reason), there was no national requirement that city buses have lifts. Every time a court ordered a transit company to put lifts on its buses, it seemed to Bill, the transit company just appealed the ruling.

The other problem with these special van services was that they could carry only a certain number of people — certainly not everyone who wanted a ride somewhere; so they "prioritized" the rides by "importance" — that is, what the bus company considered important. Doctors' appointments, not surprisingly, led the list. This irritated many wheelchair users, who got sick no more often than many people who didn't use wheelchairs. If you merely wanted to shop, you were far down on the list. In this way, many people who couldn't climb aboard buses ended up never going anywhere except to the doctor; they could never get the van.

Even though Bill's city has buses with lifts that work, when Bill gets to the store — a computer store, in his case, because he is working on a term paper and needs a new box of disks — he can't get in. The shop has two steps up to its door.

They are actually fairly small steps. But to Bill they might as well be a flight of 50, because Bill, in his motorized chair, and no "wheelchair jock" (his arms are partially paralyzd, and a motorized chair weighs a couple of hundred pounds) can't just "hop up" the steps. And he can't be lifted up, either. Besides him and his chair weighing upwards of 400 pounds, Bill doesn't want to take that risk to himself or those who would offer the service. What Bill wants is what anyone would want: merely to be able to go in and buy his disks like the ordinary college student he is. Like everyone else.

For Bill, and the millions like him, there was no law, anywhere, saying that shop had to give Bill a way to get in. No law saying even that a salesman had to, at least, come out and see what he wanted and sell him the product there at the door.

So even though there was a state curb cut law; even though his city did require lifts on its buses, even if Bill had found a way up that second curb over to the bus stop — he might as well stay home, for all the good those other accessible features offered him. He still couldn't accomplish what he needed.

Disability rights activists who had worked on state laws, and had worked with the Rehabilitation Act's requirements for nearly two decades saw that, despite all these laws, society was still closed to many disabled people, because there were large gaps where disabled people had no access at all — and no way to ensure that they'd ever get any access. To stores. To shops. To restaurants. To movie theaters. To accountants' offices. Grocery stores. Hotels. Bars. Their lawyer's office. The day care center they want to use for their kids. The gym down the street.

And to jobs.

And without this access, disabled people working for the betterment of the lives of their peers knew that disabled people would continue to be the largest group of unemployed people in this nation; the group with the highest level of poverty; the group for which one in every 12 dollars of the federal budget was spent, according to the Chairman of the Equal Employment Opportunity Commission Evan Kemp — a man in a wheelchair himself who recently pointed out the "fine line," as he put it, between his being in a high-ranking government job and living in a nursing home.

This vast amount of money was going into "dependency programs." It was being spent to keep us in special, segregated programs because we had no assurance of real access to society, including jobs and everyday life, because of the gaps like Bill experienced. Many, ṃany of us wanted to work. But many businesses had no requirement to hire us. Like the blind Harvard graduate who was refused job after job; like Joe Gibney of New York, who, armed with a law degree and a business degree from a prestigious East Coast business school, applied to over 80 firms in the summer of 1990 and was turned down because he was "handicapped" and in a wheelchair, we had no legal recourse. Because, although federal contractors were supposed to "not discriminate," there were many businesses who didn't come under that law. There were gaps, huge gaps, because many companies simply wouldn't consider hiring us.

To get rid of these gaps, to give disabled people a fair chance at living in society— " a level playing field," as they put it— Congress passed the Americans with Disabilities Act in 1990.

Many, many people like Bill worked hard to get the Americans with Disabilities Act through Congress. The bill was before Congress for two sessions before it became a law. "Although that's a fast process from Capitol Hill's perspective," says the Disability Rights Education and Defense Fund's Patrisha Wright, one of the leading lobbyists for the bill, "it seemed a slow process for many of us who had been waiting for a lifetime for integration." Many, many organizations made up of people with many different kinds of disabilities, from blindness and deafness to paralysis and brain injury and mental disabilities, worked on the law to ensure that it would offer clear guidance to businesses on what precisely they had to do to open their businesses up to all of us in society. That is why so many of us were surprised and saddened when we heard many businesses and lobbyists call the law "vague."

The Americans with Disabilities Act is anything but "vague." The terms in the law like "reasonable accommodation" and "undue burden" already have a 15-year history from the Rehabilitation Act. These terms first appeared in national policy to enforce that 1973 law, and the terms have been further defined by the administration and the courts, so there's a large body of material that exists on precisely how to carry out such things, says Wright.

The law was really designed to help everyone — including businesses.

That point may have been lost in all of the fear and worry over a new set of federal "requirements" that many businesses have heard talk of.

This book aims to lead you through an easy, step-by-step understanding of what it is, precisely, that those of us who have disabilities need and want from society. We believe we can show you that what we really want to offer you is our own skills, our buying dollars, our understanding, our desire that your business increase its clientele. If we win, you see, you win, too. It's that simple — and we really believe that.

But we know we need to show you, as precisely as we are able, what kinds of things the law requires, and how you can go about doing those things as easily as possible.

In the pages that follow, we will introduce you to some of us who can not only explain the legal requirements but can show you why this law is so important to all of us — you included, whether you yourself have a disability or not. We will talk to you about the experiences we've had in stores, in jobs, in shops that led us to conclude that a law was needed. We believe we can show you how easy it really is to provide the services and dignity we want. And we hope we will give you some insights you haven't had before about this vast group of people once called "the handicapped" who now call themselves "people with disabilities."

People you know

Before we do, though, perhaps we should end this chapter where we began it -- talking about the people you know, or might know: The uncle with the stroke who is partially paralyzed. Your father, with his lost hearing. Your buddy with his artificial leg. Your cousin who has Down Syndrome like Chris Burke, the actor who stars in the TV sitcom "Life Goes On." Your neighbor's son with the brain injury.

Chances are, you don't think of any of them when you hear terms like "the handicapped" or "people with disabilities." Chances are they don't think of themselves, either, when they hear those terms.

Most of us think of "the disabled" or "the handicapped" as someone we don't know. Someone who's very different, maybe even "odd" in some way. When we know someone closely who happens to have some physical or mental problem, we most often say, "oh, but he's not really disabled." How many times have you found yourself doing that? Or have you heard someone like a wheelchair athlete say on TV, "I don't consider myself 'handicapped?'"

There's a fairly simply explanation as to why we do this almost without thinking: It's because we automatically consider someone "disabled" as different, funny, odd, peculiar, incapable. Read that last one again: incapable. If we know somebody who's pretty normal, pretty much like us, someone we've known for awhile, who happens to have lost a leg, or their hearing, well, then, they're still normal to us. Therefore, they're not "handicapped."

What's happened here? We see "normal" and "handicapped" (or "disabled") as opposites. You can't be disabled and normal both, we figure. We think "disabled" means "unable to do things." We often see someone in a wheelchair and figure there might be something "wrong with their mind," too.

It's OK to admit this. People who have these disabilities are certainly aware that we're doing it. It's time for us to admit it, too — and understand it.

This book, we hope, will help with understanding it. And changing it.

It is just this kind of separation — into "us" and "them" — that has let us continue to do things in our modern society like build buildings with steps and heavy doors and small restrooms; that makes us believe, instinctively, that "the handicapped" want to "be with their own kind." But it isn't really "them" and "us." It's really "we." People with disabilities are just like us. In fact, they *are* us. Any of us, at any time, can join the ranks. We could be in an accident and sustain a spinal cord injury. We could have an illness that leaves us deaf or blind. We could have a brain injury. If that happened, what would we want?

Many, many people who have experienced this, like Mike Collins whom you'll meet in the following pages, would tell you that we'd want what we want now: to be with our families, our friends, out in the community, working and playing and shopping and going to movies. All of us. One of the clearest goals of those who worked to pass the Americans with Disabilities Act was to break down the "us" and "them" and replace it with "we."

Even though the distinctions in what we all want are pretty small, it's true that in recent years people with disabilities have begun to see themselves as a distinct group in American society. They have become increasingly aware that their inability to get around in society does have to do with people's attitudes and barriers more than it does with their own body. Or, to put it another way: they are aware they could be living a much fuller life if society and business would give them access and and afford them the dignity they afford normal people. The Americans with Disabilities Act was passed by Congress to do just that.

Who is disabled?

The Americans with Disabilities Act has a definition of who's disabled that explains for us why so many different people, with different kinds of injuries, and physical and mental problems — even past illnesses and injuries that really don't affect anything much (except what other people think of them) — got included in this law.

The law's definition of who is disabled has three parts. A person is considered "disabled" if he or she either:
- has a physical or mental impairment that substantially limits one or more major life activity (such as performing manual tasks, being able to care for oneself, walking, seeing, hearing, speaking or learning or working),
  or
- has a *record* of such an impairment,
  or
- is *regarded as* having such an impairment.

If a person fits any *one* of these categories, the law protects them. This definition is comparable to the definition of a "disabled person" under other federal laws, such as the Rehabilitation Act and the Fair Housing Act of 1988; it has been in use since the mid-1970s.

Most of us with disabilities think this definition makes a great deal of sense. We know, from experience, that our problems aren't due to which category of "disease" we may have had or what specific kind of "injury" we sustained, but whether or not we are able to function in society. That's why the legal definition stresses that anyone who has a problem with a "major life activity" is considered disabled.

Those of us who have been in mental institutions and who are now functioning perfectly normally often encounter discrimination not because we can't see or hear or think or walk or talk normally but merely because of the word "mental illness." Once it's mentioned, people are frightened of us. We know that the attitudes others have about us have kept us out of jobs. And that these attitudes are based on no real inability of ours but on what others believe about us. That's why the definition of "disability" includes those people who "have a *record* of" an impairment.

And those of us who merely have something other people think "looks funny" have felt discrimination, too. Those of us who have sustained major burns and now have scars know the fear and turning away other people feel. The Los Angeles television newswoman Bree Walker knows it, too. The "disability" Walker has is a condition in which her hands are fused together. Not considered attractive, but they aren't a functional problem for Walker. Yet in the summer of 1991, Walker was accused, on a talk radio show in Los Angeles, of being irresponsible for daring to become pregnant with a child who might also have this disability. For Walker and her husband Jim Lampley, another Los Angeles television news personality, the ordeal left feelings of anger and rejection. "I felt as though my pregnancy was being terrorized," she told reporters.

In the early years of Walker's career, in New York television, she was told to wear fake "normal looking" hands. With the fake hands on, she really *was* "handicapped": she could not use her real hands. But her bosses wanted that, because then she looked "normal." Was that discrimination? It certainly was. It was based on no real problem, but only on a belief that her "ugly" hands could not be tolerated in view.

And that, say people with disabilities who have been though similar experiences, is why the Americans with Disabilities Act includes in its definition people who are "regarded as having an impairment."

What to call us?

Because we are painfully aware that people do consider us

"incapable" and forget that we're just normal folks, many of us have fought to have ourselves called "people with disabilities" rather than "the handicapped" or "the disabled." We don't like the "the's." It seems like just another little way of saying we're not really people. It's a small matter, but like many things you'll read in this book, it's one of the many ways that are easy, take no time or money, that add dignity to someone who for too long has not been treated with dignity.

There are other terms people use that aren't dignified, either, and you won't find them in this book:

- We don't say "wheelchair-bound" or "confined to a wheel-chair." Wheelchairs, in fact, liberate us. We resent those terms. We say, "uses a wheelchair." Please follow our lead.
- We aren't "victims" or "afflicted." We may *have* cerebral palsy; we're not a "victim of" it or "afflicted by" it. We'd appreciate it if you wouldn't use these "pity-evoking" terms, either.

Throughout the book, you'll notice places where the word "Deaf" is capitalized. Many deaf people, especially those born without hearing and who use American Sign Language, consider themselves part of a subculture in this country. They identify themselves as part of that subculture by capitalizing "Deaf." Like people who use the term African-American with pride, these people have a lot of what they call Deaf Pride and rejoice in their culture. To respect this, we capitalize "Deaf" when we use it with this meaning.

As for "handicapped" versus "disabled": The Americans with Disabilities Act uses the term "disability" as do most groups today, simply because, like the term "Negro," which was replaced by "black," the term "handicapped" is pretty much out of style. There are more "political" reasons offered by some people in the disability rights movement, but this should suffice: It's what people want to be called today.

Or, as the old joke might go: Don't call me "handicapped," call me Bill.

"Bill" is made up. But the people you'll be meeting next are very definitely real.

Chapter 1
What discrimination looks like

"When we go to a hotel, they'll tell my husband and me, 'We have an accessible room for you!' They have installed a wider door, and taken out some shelving, but that's usually it. They never have an accessible shower I can use. They never have a raised toilet seat. The phone hookups are generally all the way across the room, not by the bed. The phone is totally useless for me once I'm in bed. I'd like to know I could at least call for help from the bed if something happened to my husband, like if he had a heart attack in the night."

"I'd like to just be able to check into a hotel room and take a shower and go to bed like everyone else. But I can't."

Meet Deborah Gately McKeen. She uses a wheelchair, having had polio as a child. A counselor and psychotherapist by training, right now she's looking for a job in Tucson, where she and her husband, an electrician, recently moved. In Hyannis, Massachusetts, McKeen worked for an organization known as the Cape Organization for the Rights of the Disabled, or CORD. She was working for CORD when the Americans with Disabilities Act was signed.

Most of my life," McKeen says, "I have dealt with very patronizing, well-meaning but condescending attitudes on the part of people who in their wildest dreams couldn't imagine that I am a complete and whole person.

"Part of who I am may be connected with my disability. But a large part of it is not. I'm pretty self-analytical; I've had to be. Plus, it's part of my training as a counselor. As a younger person, I would think, 'It's because I'm disabled that I can't do this or that.' Later it dawned on me that no, it's not my disability that's causing me a problem, it's the barriers I'm facing. It's the society that's 'handicapping' me.

"I'm part of society, too. As far as I'm concerned, it's an absolute requirement that all people have an equal opportunity in our society. I'm part of that society, too. I pay taxes. And even if I didn't," she adds quickly, "people should still be treated equally. Access is a consideration we should make for any human being."

McKeen has met her share of discrimination. For her, like most people in wheelchairs, dealing with " the little indiginities," as she calls them, has been a part of everyday life — and the best thing about the new law, she thinks, is that maybe someday, when enough businesses make things accessible, like restaurants, motels, stores and rest-rooms, she won't always have to encounter the "little indignities."

Meet Amy Hasbrouck, Director of Education and Advocacy at the Boston Center for Independent Living. "I'm legally blind," Hasbrouck explains, "which means I have about ten percent normal sight. I can't describe how what I see — and what I don't — is different from what you see, because I've never seen any differently than I do now. I grew up with my disability, and I've adapted all my life. And that means I'm going to do things differently than someone who used to have normal vision but lost most of their sight later in life.

"I can read normal-size print with my glasses, but I want to stress that a lot of people with low vision *can't do that*. I want to stress that almost everyone with some — but not total — vision loss is different in what they can see. I have difficulty seeing far away. I have trouble seeing signs; in recognizing peoples' faces individually."

"Little indignities" have plagued Hasbrouck all her life, too. And they seem to be such simple things, so easily corrected. For Hasbrouck, like the millions of people with low vision, these easily-corrected things make up the frustration that comes with the disability.

These things are things the Americans with Disabilities Act considers "discrimination."

"Most of the discrimination is really subtle," Hasbrouck says. A typical example is "when I go into a restaurant, like a fast food restaurant. The menu is posted up on the wall, and I can't see it. I ask the people taking the orders to read the menu, but they don't want to. I ask, 'What do you have?' But they act impatient. 'Oh, sandwiches and stuff,' they say. They don't want to take the time to read it. And there isn't any printed menu available, like there could be. There could just as easily be one in large print." Even though Hasbrouck can read regular print, large print would work for many more people — and she could use it just as well. And she knows there wouldn't be any real difficulty in a fast food outlet having some quick-printed menus available. Nor would it be hard for an employee to take the time to read the menu. "It requires patience," says Stan Greenberg, who's totally blind.

But neither of these accommodations is provided very frequently for either Hasbrouck or Greenberg or the millions of people who can't read menus easily. Over and over, you'll hear the same theme: people who have disabilities find themselves treated as though they're a bother, that they're too time-consuming, that their desires aren't worthwhile. They're made to feel like they're the problem — when the real problem is the business or program that has failed to give them a decent way to "access" the business's products or services.

Meet T. J. Monroe and Connie Martinez. Monroe, considered "retarded," is involved with a national organization called People First. Many people like Monroe chafe at being called "retarded." Those who have been active in working for their own rights have started using the term "self-advocates" to describe themselves. "A lot of times people don't ask us how we feel." A "self-advocate" from California, Connie Martinez echoes Monroe's statements. What would she tell people about the desire for equality? "I would tell them that, if something happened to them, they'd want to be treated the same as before." "They don't want to bother with us," says Monroe.

That's the core of what the Americans with Disabilities Act considers "discrimination."

Steve Weiner has felt it, too. Deaf from birth, Weiner runs the Careers Institute at Gallaudet University, the nation's only liberal arts university for deaf people. Weiner finds it frustrating that places that should know better — universities who receive federal dollars and so have been under the requirements of the Rehabilitation Act since the 1970s not to discriminate against disabled people — refuse to provide an interpreter for him. "There's an informal group of career center directors of colleges and universities in the Washington area," he says. "We meet three or four times a year. I have asked my colleagues" — repeatedly, he says — "to at least provide an interpreter for me when we meet at one of their places. They always tell me 'it costs money' or 'it's not in the budget' or 'our vice president won't approve it.' So I usually have to bring one from Gallaudet with me. I've warned them, though," says Weiner, "that now that the ADA has passed, when there's a meeting scheduled I expect an interpreter to be made available to me."

Weiner says that he plans to file a complaint under the new law if an interpreter is not forthcoming at the group's spring meeting in 1992.

Weiner will be well within his rights if he does decide to file a complaint this spring.

Marilynn Phillips, who uses a wheelchair and is a professor at Morgan State University, has filed complaints under the Rehabilitation Act, as well as Maryland's Human Rights Law, for lack of access to many places in Maryland. Over the past few years, she has filed more than 20 complaints, from places like art museums, who receive federal dollars funnelled through the Maryland State Arts Council, who have buildings with no ramps and inaccessible restrooms, to stores like Casual Corner who have failed to obey the state's human rights prohibition against discriminating against people with disabilities by having dressing rooms she can't get into and use.

So far, she's won all of her cases. So has Gregory Solas, a former ironworker injured in a fall on the job who now uses a wheelchair. Like Phillips, Solas has used state laws and the Rehabilitation Act to gain access to places, like his daughter's school, which, as he put it, "should have been made accessible a long time ago."

"We pay taxes like everybody else and we should have the same rights," says Solas.

People like Solas and Phillips will use the Americans with Disabilities Act to gain access that they have won by law to a society that they say has not provided them with access when they have asked, over and over. So will people like Weiner and Hasbrouck.

What is the thinking of someone who files such lawsuits? Are they out there to destroy businesses? Far from it, says Solas. "I like to address issues like a gentleman, without friction. But if it comes to where you have to use the force of the law, so be it. I believe that down the road they'll convert and understand this was right. They'll realize they didn't understand."

It's not funny

"I've had cerebral palsy all my life," Comedian Geri Jewell tells a group of journalists and students. "All my life people haven't known what to do with me: 'She should be in special education.' 'No, she should be in regular school.' 'No, she should be in a school for the deaf.'" Her audience laughs. Many of us have had similar experiences.

"Today, I can pull into a 'handicap parking space,' and people start yelling at me before I can even get out of the car: 'Get out! Don't you know those are for people who are *really* disabled?!' But I can pull into a regular parking space, and people yell at me, 'Get out! You have your *own parking space.* Why do you use ours?!'

"Some people think I'm drunk." Picture her, she says, in a 7-Eleven at 7 o'clock in the morning, buying the big cup of coffee: "Somebody walks up to me and says, 'Hey, kid, it's going to take a lot more coffee than that to sober *you* up.'" Some people, she says, "are very rude, very obnoxious; they put me down. Sometimes they're very concerned about my alcohol problem; they invite me to their AA meeting." Or they think she's on drugs — "cocaine, usually, because I'm so hyper.

"Still others think I'm mentally retarded and patronize me. They talk to me like I'm five years old: *'Are You HAV-ING a GOOD Day?'* Even if I were retarded, I don't deserve to be talked to that way."

On a business flight once, she says, she had arranged in advance to have a skycap with a wheelchair meet her to get to her connecting flight because, even though she does walk, "long distances wear me out. When I have to get somewhere fast, by the time I get to my destination to do whatever I'm supposed to do, I'm wiped out." When her flight arrived at the hub airport on this particular trip, she says, sure enough there was a wheelchair waiting for her. It turned out her connection was 3 hours late — "I could have easily walked to the gate. But nobody talked to me. They got the chair, they put me in the chair, they rolled me to 'Unattended Children's Services.' They rolled me up to a table with coloring books and crayons. And the flight attendant came over to me and she said, *'Do You Have Your TICK-ET?'* I said, 'Yes.' She said, *'We're Going to HOLD It For YOU Until Your PLANE Comes.'* And I said, 'Well, alright.'"

This kind of talk continued, says Jewell, and she was really bothered by it. "She thinks I'm retarded," Jewell thought. Finally she went up to the flight attendant, but before she could say anything, the flight attendant started. *"I'm Really Glad You Came Up. I Have Something To Tell You. Your Flight is Going To Be FIVE HOURS LATE. Do You Want to Call Your Mommie and Daddy?'* "

"I don't think my mom and dad even know where I am — or care," Jewell told her. "But I would like to call my husband.

"And she was so embarrassed," says Jewell. "She took a step back. 'Oh, I'm sorry!' she said. 'I thought you didn't understand!'

"I told her, 'you made an assumption — and you acted on it and did not listen. I can understand ignorance,' I said. 'I can even tolerate ignorance, and I can say, 'OK, you didn't understand.' But you weren't listening!'

"Listen to people!" Jewell tells her audience.

" 'Let me tell you a secret,' " Jewell says she told that flight attendant. " 'Even if I *were* mentally retarded, I would know that you were talking to me differently than you are talking to someone else. It's that simple. Treat me as you would treat anybody, *regardless of the disability*.' And she thanked me.

"I've learned over the years," says Geri Jewell, "that when we become fearful, we stop communicating." When people simply believe that she has cerebral palsy, they either treat her as though she's wonderful and can do no wrong; or they treat her as pitiful. These are *their perceptions*; she stresses; they're not the reality. "It is not my responsibility to go around changing what other people believe about me. If it were my responsibility," she tells her audience, "I wouldn't be here today speaking to you. I'd still be back in that 7-Eleven convincing someone that I'm not drunk."

About all those people who have formed their opinions about her, she says: "They made a decision about me. Once that decision was made, the doors were closed: 'She's drunk.' 'She's on drugs.' 'She's mentally retarded.' ' She's wonderful.' ' She's pitiful.' God forbid that I be just human!"

Jewell tells us that "disability creates a discomfort area in all of us. It's not the disability that we're so uncomfortable with, though. It's guilt and pain. The pain has to do with being human. If we can realize that pain is a part of all of us, we can have the courage to feel it, to walk through it. Then we can see people with disabilities" for who they are, as just regular people. Most of the time, though, Jewell says, we don't really "see" people with disabilities. We only see our own pain and fear about disabilities. Psychologists call this "projection."

"That's why people with disabilities have a 73 percent unemployment rate." Because of the fear and pain nondisabled society feels, it tries to protect people with disabilities. Society goes out of its way to protect people with disabilities, says Jewell, but what society is really trying to do is protect itself from the guilt and pain.

Waiting

"We have been waiting, some of us all our lives, to have access to the things that everyone else considers their birthright," says Cass Irvin, who has been active in efforts to gain rights for disabled people in Louisville for the past 15 years. Irvin is paralyzed as a result of polio, and uses a motorized wheelchair to get around. "Why would people be disgusted that, now that Congress has said we have a right to access and equality, after most of our states have said this, after our cities, in their human rights codes, have agreed that we have a right to access, that we, finally, make an effort to secure those rights?"

And yet many people, when they learn we plan to file a complaint or sue some place that refuses to give us the access the law requires, are disgusted with us. Why is that? Isn't that just more evidence that people think we don't have a right to the things they take for granted?

These questions are hard ones for many business owners and entrepreneurs to have to face. It may be hard for you, as a business owner, to admit that people like Solas, Weiner, Hasbrouck, and the other people with disabilities who will be talking about discrimination and denial of access all through this book have a valid point.

Yet how else are we to interpret the hours of testimony that Senators and members of Congress heard over the last few years from one after another of people like these you've just heard? Congress believed that these stories indicated that disabled people did indeed face discrimination — from businesses and programs serving the public, from all sorts of "public accommodations" including movie houses and restaurants, bars, museums, bowling alleys, video stores, gas stations, dry cleaners, laundromats, museums, ball parks — as well as programs like beauty and real estate schools, day care centers, soup kitchens, spouse abuse shelters, adoption agenciess, halfway houses, not to mention things like pet stores, car rental agencies, groceries, hotels, motels, tax offices, health clubs and on and on.

Patrisha Wright, Director of Governmental Affairs for the Disability Rights Education and Defense Fund, worked unflaggingly on the passage of the law for two legislative sessions — which was how long it took to come up with a bill that worked both for business and disabled people, she says. Though it was a relatively fast process, she says, she reiterates that people with disabilities have been "waiting for a lifetime for integration."

Though Wright admits that many business groups complained about the bill as it made its way through Congress, she points out that "the law was drafted in a way that really protects small businesses. The law contains the same terminology that has been used in Sections 503 and 504 of the Rehabilitation Act," she says. "And we know no company"— and no small nonprofit group, either, she adds—"which has gone bankrupt as a result of complying" with that law.

The disability community agreed in the negotiations, says Wright, "that it is not fair for a mom-and-pop grocery to have the same legal and financial obligations as a big company like IBM."

We'll see how this works out when we take a look, in our next chapter, at what the law and its rules say about what you have to do as a "public accommodation."

Chapter 2
What the Law Says

The Americans with Disabilities Act tells us that:

"Historically, society has tended to isolate and segregate individuals with disabilities, and, despite some improvements, such forms of discrimination . . . continue to be a serious and pervasive social problem.

"Discrimination against individuals with disabilities," says the law, "persists in such critical areas as employment, housing, public accommodations, education, transportation, communication, recreation, institutionalization, health services, voting and access to public services." Unlike those who have experienced discrimination on the basis of race, color, sex, or religion, it says, "people who have experienced discrimination on the basis of disability have often had no legal recourse to redress such discrimination." Remember Joe Gibney, whom we met at the start of this book? Remember the blind Harvard graduate? Remember "Bill?"

"Individuals with disabilities continually encounter . . . outright intentional exclusion," says the law. They also encounter "the discriminatory effects of architectural, transportation and communication barriers." They also encounter discrimination in the form of:
- overprotective rules and policies
- failure [of companies and programs and services] to make
  modifications to [their] existing facilities and practices
- exclusionary qualifications standards and criteria
- segregation and relegation to lesser services, programs,
  activities, benefits, jobs or other opportunities.

"Census data, national polls, and other studies have documented that people with disabilities, as a group, occupy an inferior status in our society, and are severely disadvantaged socially, vocationally, economically and educationally," says the law. A large majority of people with disabilities do not go to movies, to the theater, to sports events or musical performances; a substantial majority never go to a restaurant, a grocery store or a church or synagogue. People with disabilities report that they do not feel welcome to attend or visit ordinary places open to the public and often report fear or a self-consciousness about their disabilities as reasons why they don't participate in society, said a 1986 Harris poll. Forty percent report limitations on their activities due to the inaccessibility of buildings and restrooms; it's still common for people with disabilities to have to enter by the back door. "It is significant that the only accessible entrance to the U.S. Chamber of Commerce's National Headquarters Building in Washington, D.C. is the loading and service entry located off an alleyway," Ruth Lusher of the Architectural and Transportation Barriers Compliance Board wrote in a report prior to passage of the ADA. Lusher uses a wheelchair.

The law calls people with disabilities "a discrete and insular minority." They have been "faced with restrictions and limitations," it says, "subjected to a history of purposeful unequal treatment, and relegated to a postion of political powerlessness in our society, based on characteristics that are beyond the[ir] control ... and based on the stereotypical assumptions not truly indicative of the individual ability of such individuals to participate in and contribute to society." Television achorwoman Bree Walker, whose decision to bear a child was publicly condemned because the child might inherit her "deformity" of fused hands and whom we read of earlier, certainly knows the meaning of those words which are found at the beginning of the law.

Our nation's "proper goals," says the law, "are to assure equality of opportunity, full participation, independent living and economic self-sufficiency" for people with disabilities. The law itself notes that "the continuing existence of unfair and unnecessary discrimination and prejudice denies people with disabilities the opportunity to compete on an equal basis and pursue those opportunities for which our free society is justifiably famous." This denial, the law states, "costs the United States billions of dollars in unnecessary expenses resulting from dependency and non-productivity."

The purpose of the Americans with Disabilities Act is "to provide a clear and comprehensive national mandate for the elimination of discrimination against individuals with disabilities."

The law itself has five parts, or Titles. Title I prohibits discrimination in employment; Title II in public services — which means state and local government services. Title III forbids discrimination by public accommodations and services operated by public entities, like transportation services. Title IV provides for telecommunications services for deaf people, and Title V discusses the law's technical provisions, such as attorneys' fees and alternatives to lawsuits. Title I and Title III together affect *most of the businesses in America.*

Title I, the Employment title of the law, forbids discrimination against people with disabilties by companies with 15 or more employees. However, businesses having between 15 and 25 employees will not be held to the law until July 26, 1994. Businesses of 25 or more employees will be held to the law as of July 26, 1992. However, the Public Accommodations section of the law, Title III, has already gone into effect. Title III became effective January 26, 1992.

Title I says you can't discriminate against a disabled person who works for, or who applies to work for, your business. This book does not discuss the law's employment provisions. Appendix B lists groups who are providing training and materials on this Title of the law.

However, even if you have fewer than 15 employees and therefore aren't bound by the law's employment requirements, if you do business with the public you are still considered a "public accommodation" under the law — and you must obey Title III of the law.

As a public accommodation you must not discriminate against anyone with a disability in the goods, services, facilities and accommodations you provide. That's in the law. The law also says that any newly-constructed place of public accommodation or commercial facility must be *accessible to and usable by* people with disabilities. So must any of your facilities that undergo structural alterations.

Rules issued by the Department of Justice last summer explain these requirements in great detail — as does the analysis from the Department of Justice that accompanies the rules. Both the rules and the analysis are available, totally free of charge, from the U.S. Department of Justice (see Appendix A.) Most of the people in this book would strongly recommend that you get a copy of the rules—and read them. The rules are long and detailed. But they are understandable — and, contrary to what you might have heard, they explain pretty much every typical example of discrimination that might occur with your place of business. This book will also explain, in plain everyday examples and with examples from people with disabilities, the kinds of things that are considered discriminatory and what you can do to change them.

Of course, it's true that if someone does file a complaint against your businesses or take you to court, attorneys will end up arguing over fine points in the law and the rules. But you will be able to avoid having any lawsuits filed, we believe, if you take the points in this book to heart—particularly the information explained later on, when we get into explaining step-by-step how to ensure that your goods and services are accessible to anyone with any kind of disability.

Are you covered by this law?

The Title III rules offer a long list of the kinds of places that are considered "places of public accommodation." According to the rules, they're "facilities whose operations affect commerce." The rules list 12 categories for "places of public accommodation":

1. An inn, hotel, motel or other place of lodging except places with fewer than five rental units where the landlord lives on the premises);

2. A restaurant, bar or other establishment serving food or drink;

3. A motion picture house, theater, concert hall, stadium, or other place of exhibition or entertainment;

4. An auditorium, convention center, lecture hall, or other place of public gathering;

5. A bakery, grocery store, clothing store, hardware store, shopping center or other sales or rental establishment;

6. A laundromat, dry-cleaner, bank, barber shop, beauty shop, travel service, shoe repair service, funeral parlor, gas station, office of an accountant or lawyer, pharmacy, insurance office, professional office of a health care provider, hospital, or other service establishment;

7. A terminal, depot, or other station used for specified public transportation;

8. A museum, library, gallery or other place of public display or collection;

9. A park, zoo, amusement park or other place of recreation;

10. A nursery, elementary, secondary, undergraduate or postgraduate private school or other place of education;

11. A day care center, senior citizen center, homeless shelter, food bank, adoption agency or other social service center establishment; and

12. A gymnasium, health spa, bowling alley, golf course or other place of exercise or recreation.

Sound like your business? In order to be a place of public accommodation, a facility must be operated by a private entity, its operation must affect commerce and it must fall within one of these 12 categories, says the Department of Justice. "While the list of categories is exhaustive, the representative examples of facilities within each category are not." The Department's rules, from which the above list was taken, mention only a few examples in each category. Under the category of "social service center establishments" there would also be things like rape crisis centers and halfway houses; that retail and wholesale establishments (category 5, above) would also include bookstores, pet stores and practically any other store one could think of — even though they are not specifically listed.

The Department of Justice stresses that Congress meant the definition of who is a "public accommodation" to be extensive. It includes "sublessees, management companies and any other entity that owns, leases, leases to, or operates a 'place of public accommodation.'" They say this is true even if it's something relatively short-term; for example, leasing an office just during tax-preparing season. So if you operate any kind of a "place of public accommodation," as we've explained here, you're considered a "public accommodation" yourself, and you're responsible for obeying the law.

If you're a small operation which reports to a larger firm, like a franchise, you're covered too.

What if your business is in your home?   If you are a tax consultant, or accountant, or graphics artist, and customers come to your home, then you do, indeed, operate a "place of public accommodation." But your entire home isn't under the law — only the part of it that the public comes into for business.

What the law forbids

The law puts it this way: "No individual shall be discriminated against on the basis of disability in the full and equal enjoyment of the goods, services, facilities, privileges, advantages or accommodations of any place of public accommodation by any person who owns, leases (or leases to), or operates a place of public accommodation."

The law says you have to take "readily achievable" steps to

ensure access. You should have taken these steps by now — before January 26. If you haven't already done it, begin this process *immediately*. This book will explain how.

'Readily achievable' and 'undue burden'

What does "readily achievable" mean? The law says it means "without too much difficulty or expense." What does *this* mean? It has to do with removing barriers. You have to remove "architectural barriers" and "communication barriers that are structural in nature" *now*, in "existing facilities," says the law, as long as their removal is "readily achievable." This is how the law intended to make sure that smaller businesses didn't have to spend the same amount of money as did big corporations. What's considered to be "not too much difficulty or expense" is rightly going to be different for a tax preparer working out of her home than for McDonald's.

That's why the law itself lists *factors to be considered* in determining if removing a barrier is "readily achievable." They have to do with the nature and cost of the barrier to be removed, the overall financial resources of the facility (which include things like the size of the facility — that is, how many people are employed there), as well as the overall financial resources of the person or company responsible for that facility, and, finally, the type of operation you're running.

If these details seem confusing, it's because lobbyists wanted an ironclad guide in every situation in an area where common sense is really the best guide — and this is what they came up with by way of compromise. The Department of Justice's rules go into much more detail about these points, too. If you're nervous about this, we can't stress too much that you should get a copy of the law and the rules (Appendix A gives you information on ordering). But we also want you to recognize that people often make a "mountain out of a molehill" — and this seems to be one of the cases where it has happened. By the time you finish reading this book, we think you'll have a good sense of what "readily achievable" means in a common-sense way. We'll also suggest groups of disabled people to contact to talk it over with.

The key to remember here is that we disabled people want to be able to participate, and want you to make a real effort to let us do that.

Nobody is asking you to go bankrupt. Later on, you'll hear Lorelee Stewart explain how her tiny, nonprofit independent living center, where almost all of her staff needs various barriers removed, manages routinely to do it on a tiny budget.

The law says you have to make "readily achievable" changes to provide access, even if you can offer your service to disabled people without making the changes. For example: Let's say your front entrance has a 1-inch step. It would cost you about $50 in cement to ramp it. But, you say, "disabled people can get into my office from the back loading dock." Nonetheless, you have to ramp your entrance, since it is "readily achievable" — that is, it's neither very difficult nor expensive to do it.

There's another term similar to the "readily achievable" concept which you'll hear: that term is "undue burden." It means *"significant* difficulty and expense." The Department of Justice's rules say that you don't have to provide any "auxiliary aids and services" if it's an "undue burden" to do it. Otherwise, though, you have to provide them. (We'll explain what "auxiliary aids and services" are a little further on.)

My responsibility? Or my landlord's?

The Department of Justice's rules allow a landlord and tenant to work out, in the terms of their contract, which of the two will be responsible for taking these "readily achievable steps" to ensure access. The Department of Justice reminds us that "The ADA was not intended to change existing landlord/tenant responsibilities." They suggest that this would usually mean that a landlord can be expected to make "readily achievable changes" and "provide auxiliary aids and services" in common areas that all tenants use, as well as changing any discriminatory practices and procedures that affect all the tenants. The tenant, on the other hand, would be responsible for changes needed within her own "place of public accommodation."

Specific responsibility for these things can be spelled out in lease negotiations. But fairness should prevail. For example: if a hospital provides space for a Lamaze group to come in and teach childbirth classes, the big hospital is, in a way, profiting from the classes being there. So it seems fair for the hospital to foot the bill for something like an interpreter — rather than the group itself, who many not have funds to do it and for whom it might be considered an "undue burden."

Suppose if you offer services to the public, but don't yourself have any fixed space you use on a regular basis? For example, suppose if you're a performing artist or a consultant who does trainings, and you lease space in hotels in various cities for 2 days at a time to hold trainings in throughout the year? These are the kinds of things that the Department of Justice suggests should be spelled out by you and the "landlord" you're renting from, in the lease or space contract negotiations. Common sense, however, dictates some things. For example, it would be up to you to provide what the law calls "auxiliary aids and services" — things like, for example, training materials in braille or on tape if someone needs them — or an interpreter. Your landlord's space, which you're leasing, should be accessible in its structure.

The key for you, of course, in this case, would be to seek out a landlord who has a fully accessible meeting room or auditorium already. Don't rent space in an inaccessible hotel/conference center. If you do, a disabled attendee could hold you responsible for failing to provide your service in an accessible location — because you had another choice. You didn't have to rent that location.

(A word to savvy building owners and theater operators: the more accessible you make your spaces, the more apt you are to get bookings from public groups, who will be looking for accessible locations in which to hold their events!)

Maybe I'm exempt from the law

Are you exempt from the law entirely? The law exempts private clubs and churches — the same groups already exempt from the Civil Rights Act. Michael Collins, like others, finds this exemption frustrating: "I think religious organizations should have a responsibility, even though they are exempt from the law, to make their facilities as accessible as possible," he says. However, the Department of Justice explains that, just as with the Civil Rights Act, if a church runs a day care center open to the public, that day care center is considered a "place of public accommodation" and must comply with the law. And, says the Department, the law would kick in if a private club leases space to some group like a bar association to hold a conference.

What are "auxiliary aids and services"?

They're primarily things to make your place or program accessible to deaf and blind people — but it might include people with other physical disabilities as well. The Department of Justice's rules include qualified interpreters, notetakers, computer-aided transcription services, written materials, telephone handset amplifiers, assistive listening systems, telephones compatible with hearing aids, closed caption decoders, open and closed captioning, telecommunications devices for deaf persons (TDDs) and videotext as "auxiliary aids and services."

There may be other "effective methods" not in that list, says the Department — other methods of making things that are normally communicated by sound available to people with hearing impairments; they too would be considered "auxiliary aids and services." The list also includes similar kinds of things for folks who can't handle visual materials: things like qualified readers, taped texts, audio recordings, brailled materials and large print materials.

What are "qualified" interpreters and readers?

Notice the word "qualified" appears in connection with both "readers" and "interpreters." There's a reason for that. Too often deaf and blind people have had to rely on people pressed into service for them who aren't really good at it, and thus have had to get second-rate communication. For example: people who happen to know a little finger-spelling really can't adequately interpret something like a public hearing or a tax seminar when the deaf attendee is herself fluent in American Sign Language — which is its own language with its own grammar, syntax and rich set of meanings. To deprive someone like this of a "qualified" interpreter is discriminatory, says the law. Another situation deaf people often find themselves in is having to rely on a family member to interpret for them — somone who does know sign language but who may be emotionally biased. Using such an "interpreter" is totally inappropriate. One couple in marital counseling — he deaf, she hearing — had to rely on the hearing wife to interpret the counselor's discussions with the husband about the failing marriage! This was clearly an "inappropriate" situation. This is not allowed under the ADA. The interpreter has to be a neutral third party.

We'll talk about "auxiliary aids and services" more when we discuss how exactly to go about making your place and services accessible in our chapter, "All About Auxiliary Aids and Services."

Avoiding that "undue burden"

Remember the "undue burden," above? Though disabled people want access desperately, they really don't want to hurt business. That's something you've got to believe.

It's pretty unusual, to say the least, that a group of people who have been discriminated against, who have one of the lowest income rates in the nation, who have been excluded systematically from much of society, would be concerned about businesses suffering from having to spend money on them. But they are.

People with disabilities who have worked in this area for years point out, over and over, that most of the changes they need *don't* require "too much difficulty or expense." The large-print menus Hasbrouck spoke of in our last chapter might cost you $5 for 10 or so at a quick-print shop. They'd cost even less than that generated with the laser printer of your office computer. They would certainly cost far less than many of those throw-away pamphlets now available in many fast-food chains explaining calories, nutritional facts and what the chain is doing to help the environment.

The Job Accommodation Network exists as a free service, with a toll-free number (1-800-526-7234) to explain to businesses exactly how to find these easy solutions. The 10 Regional Disability and Business Technical Assistance Centers funded by the federal government to help you comply with the law are also free. These centers are listed in Appendix B.

Barbara Judy, director of the Job Accommodation Network, explains that the service was set up as a part of the President's Committee on Employment of People with Disabilities back in 1984. "We wanted a source of information on what had been done by companies to hire or retain a person with a disability." They knew the knowlege was out there, says Judy. "We collected information from the businesses we were already involved with at the President's Committee," she says. "From there we added information for products on things specifically for people with disabilities" — like braille personal printers or TDDs — "or things commonly in use in the workforce. For example, tape recorders are pretty standard in business. Ones with big push buttons are available. So are ones that are voice activated. They're pretty standard products today. So if someone calls us and has an employee who needs a voice-activated one, we can tell them who makes these products."

The work at JAN is done by telephone consultants, the majority of whom are themselves people with disabilities. They work from an internal database of over 4,000 products and sources which is constantly being updated. JAN's consultants, says Judy, are trained in "discussing what can allow a person to function." Once you've talked with local people with disabilities about changes you need to make, JAN may be a good source to locate the products you need.

Judy, like Wright before her, points out that they've had experience working with folks who for nearly 2 decades have had to comply with the Rehabilitation Act. She stresses that the information you need to accommodate a person with a specific disability has been done by others before you. The information on how to do it — often inexpensively — is out there. JAN can put you in touch with it as well as with someone who has done it. The best part may be that the Job Accommodation Network's services are totally free to you. Funded by the U.S. Department of Labor, this group bears a call from you.

As we take a look at some specific kinds of physical changes you should make in your "public accommodation" in upcoming chapters, we'll also take a look at how much a typical change would be likely to cost.

But if we listen carefully to the people we've already met in this book, and listen carefully to the ones we're about to meet, we'll start to understand why so many of them stress that the "readily achievable" changes shouldn't cost very much: because many of the changes are simply changes in attitude.

Chapter 3
How to Stop Discriminating — for Free

Gregory Solas, a former ironworker injured on the job, now uses a wheelchair. "When I ask where the accessible restroom is, people say, 'why didn't you go to the bathroom before you came here?' Or they'll say, 'Why do you need a water fountain accessible? We'll get a drink for you.' Or, 'Why do you need a phone? We'll make the phone call for you.' Or, 'Why do you need the fire alarms lowered? We can pull the alarms for you.' These are just peoples' attitudes! Wow! What a world disabled people have been living in! It's incredible. Until you become disabled, you don't really know the score."

"I like the idea of being able to go in and out of a door without having to 'ask someone' first," adds Deborah McKeen. "Of course people will help you with it, but I am tired of having to ask. I don't want to have to ask. I want to go in and out and deal with other, more important issues in my day, like other people do."

"Discrimination happens so subtly," says Stan Greenberg. It's discrimination, nonetheless. "Three of us — all of us blind — went into a restaurant not too long ago. Each of us had our guide dog. The first thing they tried to do was to sit us out of the way — 'so our dogs would be safe,' they told us. After we convinced them that we had a right to sit anywhere (and that the issue had nothing to do with safety for anyone), they sat us around a bench, and pulled out the table for our dogs to get behind it — then they pushed in the table and squashed our dogs."

"You can't come in here. You can't be in here without 'staff.' We don't want your kind in here. What if you hurt someone?" People who are institutionalized are often distrusted, simply because they're known to be from an institution, says Lorelee Stewart, an officer of the National Council on Independent Living. Stewart calls herself a psychiatric survivor. "Attitudinal barriers" are common for people with psychiatric disabilities, says Howie The Harp, who runs the Oakland Independence Support Center, a client-run program serving mentally disabled homeless people. "Attitudinal barriers" is another way of saying discrimination. It often occurs "when someone acts unusual. People who talk loudly, or make noises, or behave in what are considered odd ways — people tend to want to get rid of them — get them out of the store, out of the restaurant, out of the theater. For example, if someone in a movie theater is talking to himself, and I'm sitting next to him, then that person is hurting my ability to enjoy the movie. But if they're just sitting there making faces, that's a different matter." As long as they're not harming anyone, or endangering anyone's safety, they have a right to be there, he says.

•••

"The major non-physical barrier people like myself face," says Frank Bowe, a professor at Hofstra University in New York's Long Island, "is the inability of most people to comprehend just how difficult it is to lipread and interact in a group" when you're deaf. Bowe is deaf. A longtime civil rights activist, Bowe has worked on various kinds of national legislation for people with disabilities since the early 1970's, at one time heading up the Washington, D.C.-based American Coalition of Citizens with Disabilities. "People tend to become upset with me if I don't seem to 'be interested' and participate in their conversations. I get accused of 'wandering off' and 'not making the effort' when in fact I've worked harder than anyone else there." After awhile, he says, he "just can't take the frustration any more" of trying to concentrate on what is by its nature an extremely difficult activity for deaf people.

•••

"The difficulty is attitudinal," says Bonnie O'Day, director of the Boston Center for Independent Living. "People don't understand how a blind person can do a job. They have difficulty conceiving of it because of their own fears," says O'Day, who is partially blind.

O'Day applied for a job as a teacher's assistant when she was in college, she says. "The teacher wouldn't hire me, because I was blind. And she said so. She said I wouldn't be able to type up her handwritten notes. When I suggested that she simply dictate onto tape, she just snapped that 'that's not the way I choose to do things!' — even though what I had suggested many people find much more efficient than writing notes. She just wouldn't do it — and that was that."

"A lot of people in the community do not think of us as a normal person," says T. J. Monroe, who's been labeled "retarded." "They don't want us in their establishments. They don't want to talk to us. We are not important to people."

People call Connie Martinez "retarded." She finds that unfair — and the label often results in unequal treatment. "There's no difference. It's just a tag we have; a tag. A person has a right to be out with everyone else. No one — no one — has a right to keep us out."

What would she tell business owners? "I would tell them not to be afraid of us. We still think. We have a mind. Ask yourself, 'why is it so easy to be prejudiced?' You're not going to get a germ from us, you know. We are just people, too."

What the law forbids

Let's look now at what the law actually forbids. You may be surprised that a lot of them don't have to do with buying, installing or building anything. The discrimination many disabled people face — and may feel they face at your businesses establishment as well — doesn't require money to change. It requires a change in attitude.

Certain activities are considered discriminatory under the law:

1. **Denying someone with a disability the opportunity "to participate in or benefit from** the goods, services, facilities, privileges, advantages or accommodations" you provide other people.

2. **Providing people with disabilities with unequal benefits** — like giving them a lesser program or service. For example, the Department of Justice tells us, persons with disabilities must not be limited to certain performances at a theater.

3. **Providing a separate, segregated service.** The law requires that disabled people be served in an integrated setting. It also protects disabled people who don't want to participate in any "special" program or service set up for them, but who want instead to simply take advantage of the regular service. They have a right to do this, says the law.

These points in the law come from a long history of disabled people being given separate services. They're usually not called "segregated" services, though. They're called "special."

Separate, segregated and "special"

"Special. Such a nice name. How nice to be special!" says Cass Irvin, who many years ago refused to use the term. "It's just another word for 'segregated.' " For years special services have been the rule for disabled people. Special buses. Special Olympics. " 'Special' is a euphemism, a word introduced by do-gooders to sugar-coat their control of our lives," says John R. Woodward of the independent living center in Tallahassee, Florida.

Most disabled people are sick of "special." That's why the law makes such a point of the fact that, even if you offer disabled people a "special service," thinking it might be better for them, they have the legal right to refuse the special service and opt for what you're offering everybody else.

An example? Many hotels have insisted that disabled people stay in a ground floor room — many of them have installed their "accessible rooms" there. A hotel guest who may look very disabled to you, however, may know that they can get along perfectly fine in a room on the top floor, whether it's "specially equipped" or not. They may want it for the view — or for whatever reasons people want various hotel rooms. Under the Americans with Disabilties Act, you, as the hotel operator, can't require them to take the "accessible room," even if you think it's better for them. In short, and not to put it too bluntly, it's not your business whether or not they can function on their own. That's their business.

By the same token, you can't force someone to come to a special showing of a movie that you've decided to offer "special" for disabled schoolkids. A disabled kid — or his parents — can come to any showing they want to. Nothing in the law, of course, prevents you from offering special programs, opportunities or services. And some people with disabilties may like that. At times, it's even appropriate: providing accessible parking spaces is required by the ADA and by many state laws. It's a separate service, one that people with heart conditions who can't walk long distances or people in wheelchairs who need space to let down their van lifts or get their chairs out of the back seat really need. Still, you can't require that someone in a lift-equipped van park only in one of these "special" access spots if they choose to park in a regular spot. Of course, they may take their chances at getting stuck in between two cars in a too-narrow spot. That's their problem, not yours.

A lot of this "special" stuff comes from the false belief that all people with disabilities need extra help. Or that people with one kind of disability — say, the inability to walk — are the same as people with another kind of disability, say, the inability to see. More than one independent blind person traveling through an airport has been forced by too-solicitous airlines staff to be carted in a wheelchair from gate to gate, when they're perfectly capable of walking.

"People give you help you don't need," says Stan Greenberg. "I was in the Denver airport not too long ago. I knew where I was in the airport, and where I was going. But suddenly someone grabbed my arm and started to propel me in a direction I didn't need to go in."

This was something Greenberg says he neither wanted nor needed. Some blind people may want only verbal directions. But you have to recognize that when you give such directions, you can't be "visual" about it. "When I'm in the airport, and ask someone, 'which way to Gate 78?' they'll often simply say, 'over there' and they point. Now I know to say, 'do you mean 'to my right?' or 'to my left?' Then they'll often say, 'whatsa matter, you blind?'" 'Yes, as a matter of fact, I am,' I tell them."

Other blind people may want more direct assistance — generally in the form of asking you to walk along with them — and they can explain to you how you can do this. The key? Ask them! The point: let us decide for ourselves what we need — and want — to do.

If Greenberg's response, above, seems a tad harsh to you — after all, a blind person should be grateful the person is willing to help at all, you think — listen to how Deborah McKeen explains the exhaustion many of us feel at always having to be "nice": "I find the day to day existence of fighting barriers both annoying and frustrating. I'm as entitled as the next person, I think, to have a bad day," she continues. "Yet disabled people are always expected to be cheery and to smile."

The law says you can't require disabled people to use *only* the special service or accommodation you've provided for them. Your goal, say people with disabilities, should be to get away from the idea of segregated stuff entirely — things like special entrances and special restrooms — and simply open your regular business or your program up to everyone. In a few chapters, we'll see ways to do this.

The story Greenberg told at the start of this chapter could be titled, "The Case of the Too-Eager Accommodationist." It's the flip side of the person who doesn't want to provide any accommodation. And it's sometimes just as bad. The restaurant's Too-Eager Accommodationists "were providing us with an 'accommodation' which we didn't ask for, which we didn't need and which turned out to be wrong," says Greenberg. "They never checked with us to find out what it was we wanted."

You can't require people with disabilities to sit in one particular place in your restaurant — out of the way of other diners, in a separate room, for example.

This issue came up more than once when people who had disabilities like cerebral palsy testified before Congress. How many times had they been told they had to sit in an out-of-the-way place so as to not disturb other diners! The law makes it clear that anyone with a disability has an equal right to participate in an "integrated" setting.

"The provision of goods and services in an integrated manner is *a fundamental tenet* of nondiscrimination on the basis of disability," says the Department of Justice. Those are our italics. We want you to understand how important the idea of integration is to disabled people.

The provisions of Title III, says the Department of Justice, "are intended to prohibit exclusion and segregation . . . and the denial of equal opportunities enjoyed by others, based on, among other things, presumptions, patronizing attitudes, fears and stereotypes."

For example, they point out, "a person who is blind may wish to decline to participate in a special museum tour that allows person to touch sculptures in an exhibit and instead tour the exhibit at her own pace with the museum's recorded tour." The law does not require the blind person "to avail herself of the special tour."

"Modified participation for persons with disabilities *must be a choice, not a requirement.* We're adding italics to that, too.

The key to learning what to do, say our experts with disabilities, is simplicity itself: ask the disabled person what he wants!

The 'safety' issue — and insurance coverage

The law also says you can't restrict someone with a disability. You can't, for example, tell someone with a disability that they can only use certain portions of the health club but not all of it. "Employees are sometimes afraid you're going to trip over a weight or hit your head if you're blind," says Greenberg. "A competent blind person doesn't have those problems," he points out. "The first thing people need to do is to treat us as though we're competent — that, if we come in to some place like a gym, then we're capable of handling the stuff in there — or of learning, just like anyone else who signs up. I've never heard of a case that a blind person can't bench press just because they're blind," he adds, laughing.

"Safety" is often a factor cited in restricting disabled people. "It's not safe for them to do this!" People with disabilities have long insisted that the "safety" excuse is based mostly on false beliefs about their abilities — the "myths and stereotypes" the law refers to over and over. The law says you cannot use the excuse of "safety" to exclude or restrict someone.

"Our insurance won't cover you!" is a frequent excuse many of us have heard when told we can't participate in a program. The Department of Justice says "a public accommodation cannot refuse to serve a person with a disability because its insurance company conditions coverage or rates on the absence of persons with disabilities." "This is a frequent basis for exclusion [of disabled people] from a variety of community activities," says the Department, "and is prohibited" by the law.

"Health insurance is also a big issue," says June Kailes, a West Coast disability consultant who used to run the Westside Center for Independent Living. Kailes has cerebral palsy. "People with cerebral palsy," says Kailes, "almost never can get health insurance." Though the law says differences in rates must be based on "sound actuarial principles," Kailes and others insist this isn't being done, and warn of lawsuits to follow. Insurers "lump everyone with cerebral palsy into one category," she says. In reality, cerebral palsy manifests itself in a wide variety of ways, she points out. "It's like saying everyone with red hair can't get insurance."

While the Department of Justice's rules say that insurers may continue to underwrite, classify or administer risks consistent with state insurance laws, they warn that things like this must not "be used as a subterfuge to evade" the purpose of the law. Congress intended to deal with insurance practices by prohibiting different treatment — unless, says the Department, such differences are "justified."

A person with a disability "cannot be denied insurance or be subject to different terms or conditions of insurance based on disability alone, if the disability does not pose increased risks," said the Senate Committee on Education and Labor. If a disabled person is denied insurance, said the Committee, it must be "based on sound actuarial data and not on speculation." They went on to point out that an insurance plan "may not refuse to insure, or refuse to continue to insure, or limit...coverage... or charge a different rate for the same coverage solely because of a physical or mental impairment, except where . . . based on sound actuarial principles." The department notes that life insurance, health insurance, property and casualty insurance all fall under the scope of the law.

Many people with disabilities told the Department of Justice that they had difficulty getting automobile insurance simply because they were disabled, even though they had good driving records. This point irritates many people with disabilities, who have, they believe unfairly, been denied things like auto insurance due to no actuarial basis whatsoever but simply due to a "belief" on the part of insurers — a stereotype.

Many disabled people have been discriminated against on the basis of safety. Besides forcing guests to take ground-floor hotel rooms because of safety reasons, people are told they can't sit anywhere but in the backs of movie houses; told they can't participate in integrated sports; told they can't go on field trips with their classmates—all under the guise of "safety considerations." Most of these restrictions, it turns out, are based on no real data but myths and stereotypes. Though a "public accommodation" may impose safety requirements, says the Department of Justice's rules, they have to be "based on actual risks and not on mere speculation, stereotypes or generalizations about people with disabilities." It would be appropriate, for example, to require that everyone on a raft trip be able to swim. But if a paraplegic says he can swim, you don't have a right to keep him off the expedition simply because he's partly paralyzed. Many paraplegics are good athletes and can swim well, as are people with other disabilities. People may simply assume such people can't swim. This is a good example of speculation in action — and it happens all the time to people with disabilities. The law now forbids that.

You can't require, either, that a disabled person be accompanied by someone else. You can't require someone to bring along their "attendant" when they attend a seminar you're offering, for example.

Carrying people vs. ramping steps

This is often offered as a solution to people in wheelchairs — but it's not an acceptable one under the law. Deborah McKeen tells of a restaurant experience she had on Cape Cod that sounds all too familiar to many of us: "We went to a restaurant and wanted to go to the bar. My friends could, but I couldn't — because the bar was up three steps." McKeen and her friends opted to sit at a table on the ground level. We wanted to order from the bar menu, which was cheaper, but they said we had to be in the bar to order from it. They said they'd carry me up to the bar, though. I said, 'Oh, no you won't; not unless you , too, will let yourselves be carried up.' " Under the ADA, it would be illegal for that establishment to refuse to serve McKeen and her friends from the bar menu. They have as much right as those people who can walk into the bar to order from its less-expensive menu.

Marilynn Phillips ran into the problem at an Ann Arbor coffee-house. "The place was not accessible." Her companions hadn't realized it beforehand, or they never would have planned to go there. "But there we were, and so they went in. They thought there might be an accessible entrance somewhere else." When Phillips asked the pro-prietors at the door if there was another entrance that was accessible, "They said, 'No, but we carry people in all the time.' I said, 'That's outrageous!' but they said, 'Well, our people understand how to do it;' they said they had another wheelchair user who didn't mind, and so on. People don't understand: this isn't 'access.' It's condescending."

Discriminatory policies and practices

The Department of Justice requires you to modify your policies, procedures and practices so you can accommodate people with disabilities. One example: changing a policy that allows only one person in a dressing room at a time; such a policy would exclude a disabled person who needs a friend to come in for assistance. Another example: changing your motel's reservation policy in order to keep your wheelchair-accessible rooms freed up for someone in a wheelchair.

As many state laws now require, the ADA requires that you allow people to be accompanied by their guide dogs, hearing ear dogs or other "service animals" (such as the dogs used sometimes by people in wheelchairs to help them retrieve things from the floor and so on).

Certain procedures that have been pretty routine in business will have to be changed because of the law — but changing them is not a costly thing. No longer can you require that a person indicate on a credit application if they have any sort of a disability, including AIDS. Nor can you require a person to provide as an ID a "valid driver's license" when the person legitimately can't get one because of a disability like blindness. Both these procedures are ones that would "have the effect" of screening out someone with a disability and they're forbidden under the law. You can't argue that these changes cost money, though — other than, perhaps, reprinting some application forms!

Charging for access

Disabled people often find that companies, restaurants and so on will accommodate them some way or other — but charge them more for it. Some groceries in old towns may have steps. They also provide a home delivery service — but they charge for it. The Department of Justice points out that if your service isn't accessible to a disabled person in any way other than this "extra" way, then you can't charge for it. Some states have already used this concept in passing laws that require gas stations to serve drivers who can't get out and pump gas themselves—but letting them get the gas at the self-service price. You can't charge more for "special" services when they turn out to be the only way a person with a disability can use your store or service.

Same services, same place, same hours

Another problem disabled people run into is finding the entrance they can use locked tight, when other entrances remain open.

"Your accessible entrance — say if it's a side entrance, has to be unlocked and open the same hours as your main entrance," says Mike Collins, and he's right — the law requires it. Applying this principle to other areas, the Department of Justice points out that things like book drops, film drops, automatic teller machines and other things like that have to be accessible — because disabled people have the same right as non-disabled people to be able to use those after-hours business services.

Check-out aisles

"It bothers me that check-out aisles in stores are usually not accessible, so I have to go around to the other side of the check-out lane by another route," says Deborah McKeen. "Then I have to say, 'Yoo-hoo! I'm over here!' so the check-out clerk notices me. Then I usually have to explain, 'No, I was after the lady in the pink sweater' — who's standing in the regular line. And the lady in the pink sweater always smiles and says, 'No, it's alright; you go ahead of me.' And I don't want that. I don't want to go in front of her, and be given special consideration. I just want to be able to go through a check-out aisle like everyone else."

The Department of Justice addresses the issue of check-out aisles for this very reason. A store with a way to provide accessible check-out aisles should have at least one of them open at any time other check-out aisles are open. "Accessible" here means wider, so shoppers in wheelchairs can get through. For example, if your express check-out aisle is the wider one (which it often is, since it's usually on the end); you should designate it as the accessible one so shoppers in wheelchairs will recognize that they can get through this aisle. The Department of Justice suggests noting that people in wheelchairs can use this aisle for all purchases, whether they qualify as "express" or not.

This is another example of the kind of *change in practice* required by the law. And, as you can see, this would not ordinarily cost any money at all. You might have to spend a few dollars installing a sign above the aisle to let people in wheelchairs know the aisle is accessible. That's certainly something that's "readily achievable," isn't it?

Classes and exams

Do you offer courses to help people learn to prepare taxes? Do you run a beauty academy? A small appliances repair school? Does the community college offer people "continuing education credits" for taking your ad agency's course in computer-aided design and desktop publishing? Do you offer a CPR course?

Any group or person who offers courses — or exams — related to getting things like real estate licenses, or things like postsecondary education, continuing education courses, professional training or trade school courses and the like has to offer the courses and give exams in a place and in a manner that's accessible to people with disabilities — or offer alternative accessible arrangements.

These courses, says the Department of Justice, must be modified so they're accessible to people with disabilities— including the place where the course is offered, and the manner in which it is offered. You might, for example, have to change the length of time ordinarily required to complete the course. You might need to modify the manner in which the course is conducted or how the course materials are distributed.

Does a deaf person want to take your course? You may need an interpreter for the classes — depending on who needs it and what they need. Remember: the interpreter has to be "qualified" to interpret the couse. This doesn't mean they have to know the course material — all they're doing is interpreting. What it means is someone skilled enough to interpret clearly complicated concepts. This would normally mean someone who's considered a "Registered Interpreter for the Deaf." (We will discuss interpreters in more detail in our chapter on "auxiliary aids.")

You may need to provide course notes on tape for someone who can't see to read regular print—or for someone who can't hold papers or turn pages well. At times, it might be more appropriate to provide a student with notes in large print or in braille. For anyone who has a home computer like a Macintosh, or who can get to a quick-print shop, large print is no problem and very little expense. Our chapter on "auxiliary aids" will explain this in more detail.

You certainly need to make sure that people in wheelchairs aren't segregated but get to sit where they want. Someone with a slight vision impairment, or someone who reads lips — as well as someone who is relying on an interpreter — needs to be able to sit where they can get the maximum out of the course. They are the best ones to tell you where this is.

You may have to see that your classroom equipment is adapted so it can be used by someone with manual impairments. A lot of times this is easier than it might seem. Richard Dodds of the Regional Business and Disability Technical Assistance Center in New Jersey tells of one client who could only type by using his tongue. Rather than any fancy high-tech equipment, says Dodds, what this client needed — and what Dodds's center rigged up for a few dollars — was a regular computer keyboard turned on its side and held in a vertical position by a wooden brace.

People like Dodds can help you. The services of his Region 2 Technical Assistance Center, like the Job Accommodation Network's mentioned at the end of the last chapter, are free. So are the services of the other Regional Centers (see Appendix B).

It's possible, too, that someone who uses a computer with a specially adapted keyboard may be willing to bring the keyboard to class with them. If they suggest this, it could be an ideal solution. However, under the law you can't *require* that the disabled person provide their own accommodation—that's your responsibility. On the other hand, if a disabled person wants to do something that makes the course more accessible to them — such as taping, or writing notes in braille — they have a right to do that. Someone may bring a portable computer along with them to the course just for this reason—you can't tell them they can't, if they're doing it to make the course accessible for themselves.

As with other things, a disabled person must be allowed to take advantage of the same service — the course — that's being offered to a nondisabled person. If they have ideas as to how they can best do that, they're within their rights under the law to use their ideas to their advantage.

Courses must be given in facilities accessible to people with disabilities, says the Department of Justice's rules. Though they allow "alternative accessible arrangements" if that's not possible, it's pretty hard to think of a situation in which an accessible location can't be found for a course, say most of the people with disabilities who were involved in this book. They suggest that people who offer such courses check hard to make sure they have an accessible location — or move their course.

The Department of Justice suggests that things like videotapes, cassettes and prepared notes are ideas for alternative accessible arrangements that can be made for a course. However, the Department also reminds you that these alternative arrangements "must provide *comparable conditions* to those provided for nondisabled individuals." If an alternative arrangement is offered for an exam, it has to be at "equally convenient locations, as often, and in as timely a manner as are the other examinations."

The exam may have to be changed somewhat, says the department, like in the length of time permitted for completion; or adapting the manner in which it is given. An exam that's normally given in the form of written questions may have to be administered orally for someone who's blind, for example, or with brailled questions (Appendix C can tell you how to put exam questions into braille.)

You have to provide "appropriate auxiliary aids" for people "with impaired sensory, manual or speaking skills." As with offering the course itself, some ways to do this are by using taped examinations, interpeters or other "effective" ways of making the material available to people with hearing impairments. Remember, it's important to find out from the person taking the exam what's "effective" for him. While a sign language interpreter might be appropriate for someone whose first language is American Sign Language, it wouldn't be effective at all for someone deafened later in life who doesn't know sign language! In such a case, of course, an ordinary written exam would probably be more appropriate.

For people with low vision, you might need to provide the exam in large print. For someone who uses braille, like Stan Greenberg, a brailled exam would probably work best — but again, you need to ask. If the person used braille, how would you, the scorer, be able to read their brailled answers? There are braille transcription services, for example — but your best answer is still to ask your student! Another blind person may prefer that the questions be read to them, or provided on tape so they can proceed at their own pace, if it's not a timed exam. The Departent of Justice stresses that a reader should be "qualifed."

People with learning disabilities may also need verbal rather than written instructions. The law doesn't require you to change things that would "fundamentally alter the measurement of the skills or knowlege the examination is intended to test." But it's also known that the way an exam is given often does more to test how skilled a person is in taking exams than in testing actual knowlege of the subject the exam is supposed to determine!

Someone who can't manually write may need a transcriber for an exam. Or they may need to use a computer with voice input, or some other method. Remember: check with them!

"Alternative arrangements must provide comparable conditions to those provided for nondisabled individuals," says the Department of Justice. For example, it points out, it's wrong to provide a regularly scheduled test in a warm, well ventilated room and test blind people in a cold and drafty basement.

Before coming up with complicated and exotic ideas on how to make your course or exam "accessible," why not check with a local group of disabled people, such as people at your local independent living center? A list by state is offered in Appendix B. Or call one of your Regional Centers (also listed in Appendix B).

Changing your attitude

Up until now, we've been looking at things required by the law that don't require any structural changes. There are still others we haven't even mentioned: Patience is one of them.

As Frank Bowe pointed out at the start of this chapter, one of the barriers he faces is simply people's "inability to understand" that it's hard to concentrate on more than one person at a time when you're deaf and nobody's signing. What Bowe doesn't mention is that while he can lipread, many deaf people can't. Only about 30 percent of what's said can really be understood even by the best lipreaders. The deaf journalist Henry Kisor recounts that, as a child trying to lipread, he once lipread "what's that big, loud noise?" as, "What's that pig outdoors?"

A little understanding on the part of hearing people, and patience, and willingness to slow down, perhaps not talk all at once, and some credit that a deaf person is indeed not "wandering off" can be very much appreciated. It's an attitude thing.

So is the attitude of people who wait tables in restaurants, who may be asked to read a menu. So it takes a little more time. So what? Time is money, you say? If you're nice to your disabled patrons, they're liable to recommend your place to dozens of their friends. Finding a place that has a good attitude is sometimes hard for a disabled person. If you do you may find yourself with more business.

A little change in the attitude of people like the maitre d' who, without asking, shunted Greenberg and his friends and their guide dogs off to a spot that didn't work at all can go a long way toward providing the integration people with disabilities want.

You might want your employees to read this chapter, too. Discuss it together. Perhaps it would be useful to make a list of things staff should do in order to be sure they treat customers with disabilities as equals: things like: being friendly; not being condescending. Maybe read some of what Deborah McKeen says. Get some people from an independent living center to make a presentation on these things to your staff. Tell them what you want to accomplish. Tell them you'd like to work on your own attitude. If working with disabled people makes you nervous, admit it. Tell them you'd like to get to know them better.

Changing attitudes costs nothing. And it's a big part of what we folks with disabilities want from you.

In the next part of this book, we'll look at removing "architectural barriers" and "communication barriers that are structural in nature."

And we'll look at those "auxiliary aids and services." What are they, exactly? Where can I get them? How do I know which ones to get, which ones to offer my clients and customers? And how much are they likely to set me back? Do I have to get them if they cost too much? We'll answer this question, too.

Chapter 4
Make It Work for Everyone --
with Universal Design

In the chapter after this one, we'll explain exactly what kinds of easy barrier removal projects you can do right now — how to do them (or who to talk to who can tell you) and what they might cost.

But don't turn to that chapter yet. First, let's discuss the *idea* of removing barriers.

"The law says I have to do it." That's one way to look at it. There's a much more positive way to look at it, though, a way that makes the job fall into place, and makes "the rules" seem nothing more than common sense.

What we're going to talk about is the idea of "universal design." "Universal design" is a very simple concept: it means designing buildings and products so they can be used by everyone. Common sense? You'd think so. But for such a common-sense idea, it's taken surprisingly long to catch on.

Designers and architects have used the model of a "6-foot able-bodied young male" as the standard for designing everything from buildings to automobiles to computer keyboards, says Ronald L. Mace, a Fellow of the American Institute of Architects and President of Barrier-Free Environments, Inc. in Raleigh, N.C. Mace, who uses a wheelchair, has been working for decades to have the design industry realize that something's wrong with this idea. "It's no wonder that what we need in this society doesn't fit that model. That standard is in fact a minority itself, and it is going to be more of a minority still as the population ages." Or, as June Kailes puts it, "Most people don't fit that mold — and if they do they're not there for long." Just watch the ads for things like arthritis medicine, sore back medicine, aching joints medicine, she suggests. Doesn't that tell us something?

Mace points out something you learned at the beginning of this book: almost everyone, when you stop and think about it, has som e minor disability — some of our closest friends and relatives actually are severely disabled, even though we don't think of it that way.

When Mace works with businessess who are remodeling or

building new buildings with access in mind, he says "they are astounded to have it brought home to them how many people have disabilities." The "43-million" statistic so often mentioned doesn't really mean anything, he says, "until I point out to them that the Arthritis Foundation, for example, has 35 million members. That makes them sit up. Sometimes they'll say, 'I have arthritis myself.' But they don't think about it, because they can still function fairly well.

"I try to bring home to them things they can't deny: We are all technically part of the disability community" that the Americans with Disabilities Act was designed to help, says Mace. "We're only a step away from it at any time."

June Kailes adds these facts to support Mace's point: "Most people have at least one family member with a disability," she says. There's an 80 percent chance that you, in an average life span, will experience some disability — a 95 percent chance, she says, that you'll have a temporary mobility impairment yourself: "A broken leg, sprained ankle, twisted knee, painful back. Most people, if they live long enough, will age into disability." A U.S. Census survey in the mid 1980s pointed out that one in every five Americans has some trouble hearing, seeing or walking or moving in other ways. Kailes says that "one person out of 10 over the age of 15 has difficulty climbing steps, walking more than 1,000 feet or carrying a bag of groceries." She also reminds us that "baby boomers are moving into middle age and beyond and are starting to experience increased incidence of disability." Finally, she makes this not-so-startling assertion: "People with disabilities and who are aging *will constitute the majority of the population within the next 30 years.*" It's clear from these statistics, she says, that "The need for 'barrier-free' or *universal* design is increasing."

So doesn't it make sense to make our buildings work for the greatest number of us, rather than for a physical standard that's really in the minority? That's what "universal design" is about. It goes beyond "accessible design" because it includes everyone.

"Some architects, designers and developers view various 'access regulations' as out of proportion to the need. They say that these regulations mandate designing for the 'worst situation.'" But, Kailes insists, "Universal design is in fact designing for the *best* situation — because it better accommodates everyone by meeting the needs of a changing population."

Current building codes calling for access for disabled people, (including the ADA's Accessibility Guidelines which come with the Department of Justice rules) are limited by the concept of "minimums," says Mace. They say, "at *least* this high, at *least* this wide". Another way of saying this is to say they're *legal minimums*. They don't tell us what would work *best* for everyone.

Though nothing in any of these building access codes says a builder can't go beyond the minimum (for example, making a door a few inches wider than the minimum required), seeing an actual number in the code — even when it's a minimum — often makes a builder simply put the lightswitch, the door handle, or whatever, right at that height. This often isn't the best height for everyone, but is merely a minimum (or maximum) requirement. Often a few more inches will help millions more people. We'll explain this in a few minutes.

This approach taken by building codes has, says Mace, "unfortunately reinforced the idea of just a few accessible features in a few places — just one accessible entrance, just one accessible restroom. Instead, they could simply be making doorways and restrooms universally accessible." The "minimum" approach, Mace says, has given us *some* access, but nowhere near *universal* access". Access advocates like Mace have "been pushing up those minimums for 25 years now," he says. Now, though, he points out, "we have a nondiscrimination law — Americans with Disabilities Act — that says its discriminatory to maintain property that people cannot use. Now it becomes a moral issue for design firms, product designers and the industry."

Here are four basic ideas that make up the new thinking of universal design. Read and understand them, say advocates of universal design, and the legal access requirements of the Americans with Disabilities Act will be easy to follow.

1. Don't think 'Special'

"Special" means separate and different. It means "segregated." Remember: the ADA calls for "integration." People with disabilities don't like coming in the back door by the loading dock or having to use separate restrooms and water fountains any more than blacks did back in the days when *that* was the law of the land.

In new construction, integration is pretty much required today. But we want to suggest some more ideas, *for your current building:*

✔ Make your main entrance usable to people in wheelchairs by a ramp. If you think the price your concrete contractor charges is high, talk to a carpenter about an attractive deck-style wooden ramp. The statement you make by opening your main door to everyone will go a long way toward increasing your business among disabled people in your community. Worried about space for a ramp? There's no law that says you need steps, too. Put that ramp over those steps!

✔ Are your men's and women's restrooms next to each other, both too tiny for someone in a wheelchair? See our section on restrooms and try Ron Mace's idea of a family restroom by turning them into one, larger restroom everyone can use.

✔ Don't install an additional, "special" lower public phone for disabled people. Move your regular phone down, and add a narrow, 6-inch bench for tall people to sit down when they dial—one that doesn't obstruct someone in a wheelchair from getting up to the phone. Buy a $200 TDD machine; if you can't install it in the phone booth; put an obvious sign on the phone to tell a deaf person where to ask for it (at the cashier's counter, etc.)

Remember: think in terms of making your place easy to use for *everyone,* whether they see, hear or walk — or not.

In general, avoid "special" items like automatic door openers designed "for the handicapped" and instead buy the industry standard items that can work for everyone. You can save money, too, by avoiding things like the "special" lavatory sinks. *Do* purchase sinks that people in wheelchairs can get up to and use easily; (see the ADA's Accessibility Guidelines); *do* purchase lever-type faucets. But you don't have to pay more from medical suppliers for "special" plumbing. Any plumbing supply place can show you a range of items that work.

Other ways to avoid special is to avoid the kinds of changes in level that are so popular in trendy clothing boutiques and bar-cum-restaurants. New buildings with level changes like this will have to provide access to all these areas via ramps. If you must have changes in level, forget about steps altogether and just use ramps.

2. Create easy, *independent* access

"Our nation's proper goals regarding individuals with disabilities," says the Americans with Disabilities Act, "are to ensure . . . full participation [and] independent living." The lack of independence, as we saw in our previous chapter, is something that frustrates most of us with disabilities. Too many aspects of "access" today, though they may accomplish the task of letting people get into your place and get served, still don't allow people to do it independently.

In their effort to provide businesses with a great amount of flexibility, Congress didn't require measures that were costly or unduly burdensome. Congress allows, for example, for a waiter to read a blind diner a menu rather than providing a large-print or braille menu. While few people would object to being read a menu, a little thinking about this procedure makes you realize that it's less independent a method for the diner. It makes the diner "dependent" on someone else.

This can't be helped in many cases. Nevertheless, when possible, your goal — much appreciated by disabled patrons — is to allow independent access. If you can afford the $5 or $6 to run to a quick print place and have your menu enlarged by photocopier to a large-print size, the solution offers more independence for those diners who can take advantage of this access option.

Stan Greenberg talks about grocery shopping — independently. There are two ways to do it, both legal under the ADA. "I can go up to the courtesy desk and ask for a clerk to accompany me. In the best of all possible worlds," he says, he'd be able to do this independently. Shelves would be equipped with data codes that a hand-held scanning device could "read," telling the customer via electronic voice what item the shelf contained and the price. The technology to do this, of course, is available; it's the same technology used at the check-out counter; the only thing missing is the hand-held scanner for the blind person. Some stores will be moving to this technology in the next few years to allow blind customers the same degree of independence sighted shoppers have — to dawdle in the aisles, to comparison shop, to go back and forth in the store. Now most blind people use a sighted companion. Under the ADA, a store should provide this. What Greenberg wants, he says, is "a clerk who will show me where stuff is, who will read the labels, who will stand by me and wait and not hurry me and not make decisions for me." Greenberg, who wants the same degree of independence as a sighted shopper, says, "Most of the time when I ask the store, they do it, but I have to wait for long periods of time. I've been asked to come back when they're not busy, when a non-disabled shopper can shop whenever they want."

What Greenberg is after is independence. Providing independence should be your goal in accommodating people with disabilities. "Many places have cash registers that have the ability to speak prices aloud; that technology came along nearly a decade ago. But many stores have turned off the vocal mechanism on their cash registers," says Greenberg. "They said it bothered customers."

If you use a cash register, it's time to check with your dealer to see if you can turn its voice on — or add a voice to it. It will add to independence for blind people. The cash register that "talks" is an example of universal design: it works for everyone.

3. Make It Work for Everyone (or try to)

Use common sense. Go beyond the minimum. Install a phone in a way that the greatest number of people can use it. Put in the kind of door that the greatest number of people can get through independently. Add a door handle everybody can manipulate.

The minimum wheelchair space requirements in the ADA's Accessibility Guidelines are too tight, Mike Collins points out, for people with the new syles of wheelchairs today, which are low and stretched out, or some of the 3-wheel scooters. The law allows a toilet stall to be 36 inches by 60 inches . As you can see by measuring such a space yourself, this doesn't give a wheelchair user space to manuever. You can roll into a space this size — but you can't do anything in it.

Of course, it's a "minimum." The ADA accessibility guidelines don't say that it can't be bigger. But we ask that spaces in restrooms be 60 inches by 60 inches. That is what we call an *optimum*.

In its requirements for constructing new public restrooms, the ADA Accessibility guidelines require that one toilet stall be 60 inches by 60 inches. And, in restrooms that will have 6 or more stalls, the Guidelines say that a second accessible stall be installed with inside measurments of 36 inches by 60 inches. To understand the reason for this, read about Ron Mace's "Universal Toilet Room," below.

Another optimum concerns a "reach range." The Guidelines say that "the maximum high forward reach allowed is 48 inches . . .[and] the minimum low forward reach is 15 inches." We say the best solution is to install everything like paper towel dispensers, light switches, phones — that is, the "business part" of any equipment customers or disabled employees are likely to use — at a point where somebody who can't move *any* part of their body easily can still reach it. That turns out to be anywhere from about 35 to 42 inches off the floor — the height that your arm would be at "naturally" if you were sitting in a wheelchair with your arm resting on the armrest of the chair. That's an *optimum* reach range. It's a point that everyone can reach — even children.

"Maximums" and "minimums" have had a tragic side effect: Some builders in a hurry read their codes too quickly, and don't think. They see that "the maximum high forward reach allowed is 48 inches," and the "48 inches" part sticks in their mind. They forget that this is a *maximum*. They install the lightswitch *at 48 inches*. If you don't have good use of your arm, you can't reach that when you're sitting in a wheelchair. It's totally inaccessible at that height to people who don't have good use of their arms. The code doesn't require it be that high, of course. The code requires that the switch be *no higher than* that. What we need is an optimum. The *optimum* is anywhere from 35 to 42 inches.

We subtitled this section, "or try to." Another way to say this is, "Do the best you can do." We want you to go beyond the minimums and maximums where you can — to do the best that can be done. But we also want you to know that, in making "readily achievable" changes in your present situation, the law gives you leeway to "do the best you can." When you alter your place or start new construction, you must follow the ADA Accessibility Guidelines. But nothing says you can't go beyond them to the *optimums* we've discussed.

"In new construction there shouldn't be any problem," Mace reminds us. "Renovation is another matter. That's why the guidelines for the law are flexible. They want you to do what's do-able."

4. The Principle of "The Most Disabled User"
Don't be surprised if a disabled person tells you "you don't have to do that much." She may be right — when it comes to *her* alone. Most of us with disabilities have for so long had to be grateful for the very

tiniest bit of access that many of us have learned to think in very personal terms, and the most limited ones, too. If I have a tiny wheelchair and can get through a 28-inch doorway, I may tell you that your 28-inch doors are "fine" and that you don't have to do more. But that advice, even if offered in good faith, would still be wrong. In the same way, many wheelchair "jocks" and people with powerful, motorized wheelchairs do not need ramps with a 1:12 slope (sloping out 12 inches for every inch of height it must span). Many people cannot use ramps independently with a slope steeper than that — though folks you talk to may be able to. (The solution in new construction is to avoid changes in level altogether . Make it flat!)

When someone tells you what they need for access, you might find it useful to ask them: "Will this work best for people *even more disabled* than you? If I make it work for *the most disabled user*, will it still work for you?"

This principle doesn't always work. Even if you make your place accessible to someone who seems the "most disabled" in terms of deafness — someone who is totally deaf — you won't necessarily ensure access for everyone who's just hard-of-hearing. While providing a TDD may work, people who are hard of hearing may need phones with built-in amplifiers instead. Nobody they know uses a TDD; giving them one would be useless since they'd have no one to call. In the same way, a sign language interpreter can't provide "access" for a deaf person who doesn't know sign language.

Still, when providing changes in your str*ucture*, the principle is one that it's wise to keep in mind. Things like automatic doors make life easier for everyone. If you can offer automatic doors — not special ones but the regular kind found in groceries and hotel parking lot entrances — people with disabilities will love you for it.

An Important Note: "Almost" Isn't Good Enough

If a person's wheelchair is 30 inches wide, it won't go through a 29-inch door. It just won't.

"We tried to make it accessible!" said one frustrated restaurant owner we know when a patron in a 31-inch wheelchair complained he couldn't use the restroom. The owner had remodeled his restroom for access. "It's almost wide enough!" moaned the frustrated owner.

But "almost" wasn't good enough. The restroom was as inaccessible to this patron as if no remodeling had been done at all. This owner had not done his remodeling in compliance with the building code. He had it done before the ADA. His state building code's access provisions called for wider doors, but he did the job himself and he wasn't familiar with the codes. He did his best, but it didn't help this patron who had to use the toilet. A even sadder footnote: The wheelchair-using diner had selected this restaurant because a friend had told him it had recently remodeled its restroom for access! That's why we stress that, when making accommodations for disabled patrons, your aim should be to create *universal* access.

Another place that "almost" isn't good enough is with ramps and curb cuts. If there's a lip at the bottom, some people won't be able to use it at all by themselves. That 1-inch lip might as well be a foot-high curb, if they're going to use it independently. When you make your "readily achievable" changes, remember: Go beyond "almost."

A word to the wise: you (or your contractor) mu*st comply with* the ADA Accessibility Guidelines *when remodeling or building new structures*. Doing it yourself is no excuse for not knowing the technical requirements. Nor can you use the excuse that a disabled person gave you incorrect advice, and expect to be let off the hook if somebody later comes along and sues you because you're not accessible. (To get your free copy of the Accessibility Guidelines, see Appendix A.)

Going Beyond Minimums — to Optimums

1. Put everything at optimal wheelchair-users' reach — at the level they can reach it even if they don't have much arm movement. We suggest an area between 35 and 42 inches from the floor.
2. Give wheelchair users a 60-inch by 60-inch space to maneuver in.
3. Put in automatic doors — or lighten your doors so that it takes no more than 5 pounds of force to open them.
4. Make doorways 36 inches wide.

These examples are just the start of ways you can think of to make your place work for everyone.

Do it right — the first time . . .

"The problem isn't so much the cost but the not knowing. People are afraid of the unknown. I've had companies say to me, 'We want to do it right. We don't mind paying for it, but we want to do it right the first time and not have someone come back later and say we did it wrong and now we have to redo it,' " says Ron Mace.

That's what happened to our frustrated restaurant owner. He thought he was doing the right thing.

When you alter your place, whatever new you add or change must comply with the Accessibility Guidelines of the ADA if it affects the *usability* of your place. "Usability" is the key word here. If you paint a room, you don't automatically have to make that room accessible. But if you move an electrical outlet, says the Department of Justice, "the new outlet must be installed in compliance with the ADA Accessibility Guidelines." People *use* electrical outlets; changing one affects *usability*.

Get a copy of the Department of Justice rules on the ADA — we've suggested this before. Now we're suggesting it again. In the back of the rules are the ADA Accessibility Guidelines. When you're doing any remodeling, show them to your builder. Or, if you're handy at do-it-yourself projects, read them yourself. Look up the item you want to change — a restoom, an entrance, a phone booth. The Guidelines will list the specifications that work for most people.

Remember: You are *required by law* to follow these Guidelines when you're doing alterations and new construction. We add this suggestion: think in terms of *universal* design and try for *optimum* access.

. . . And gain some economic benefits

Kailes gives some sound reasons as to why *universal* design works so nicely. "Wide doors and hallways make moving furniture easier. Adjustable counters and storage spaces are not only helpful to wheelchair users but also benefit people who prefer to sit" while doing things like chopping vegetables or filing.

Developers often complain that ramps take up valuable real estate; but Kailes points out that ramps *aren't necessary at all* in new construction if entrances are merely placed at grade level. "Stairs are not required, but ramps are," she says, referring to the law. The point is you don't need both, she says. "It is steps that are unnecessary, hazardous and expensive."

Kailes has also heard builders complain that bathrooms and kitchens that can easily accommodate someone in a wheelchair use up too much square footage. "The extra space makes a great place for storage and work islands," she says, "that can easily be removed when more space is needed."

Kailes says owners often resist universal design because they think it will look "special" or impose strict restraints on a designer's creative process. "Some builders equate 'access' with 'ugly' and with having to respond to a small but loud and fanatical group of people with disabilities."

Instead, she says, look at it this way: "Think about universal design on a personal level. Will your home or shop or store be adaptable for a lifetime" of work there for you and your employees? Will you be able to take advantage of any customer who wants your service? If you follow universal design principles, it will.

Two Fine Examples of Universal Design

The Case for Automatic Doors

One of the most frustrating aspects of being disabled is having to wait for someone to hold open a door for you.

"Automatic doors give me an opportunity to go in and out at my own discretion," says Debbie McKeen. "Otherwise I have to sit and wait, and ask someone, 'please hold the door for me?' and then they do, and so I smile, and we all have to make little jokes about running over toes and so on, and I thank them — but sometimes I'd just like to not have to be dependent and just go in and out of a mall or a store like everyone else and not have to engage a stranger for help."

Like Stan Greenberg who would prefer to grocery shop with a scanner, like many people who'd prefer to read braille menus to having a waiter read it to them, automatic doors give us all the same kind of independence. They truly make us equal.

Automatic doors make life easier for everyone. They're routine in groceries and at hotel baggage loading areas — to make life easier for grocery shoppers and bellhops. Why then, say an increasing number of people with disabilities, can't automatic doors become routine?

"How many new malls use heavy glass doors?" asks Michael Collins. "Yet you go to your local grocery, and you can get in and out. The convenience of automatic doors has been proven worldwide," he insists. "Yet designers and architects keep using heavy glass doors because they think they're more 'aesthetic.' If you can't get into a place, it makes no difference how 'aesthetic' it is — you can't use the services inside anyway."

"You don't have to be disabled to appreciate automatic doors," says Barbara Judy of the Job Accommodation Network. Shoppers with packages, parents with baby strollers, business executives with briefcases and tubes of sales displays, deliverypersons like the people from UPS all benefit from automatic doors. In Kyoto and Tokyo, Japan, automatic doors are common in restaurants, convenience stores and even McDonald's. It's time they became universal.

No, the new law doesn't require an automatic door. But when you remodel your entrance, plan a new addition or build a new place, why not make an automatic door part of your building plans anyway?

Are they expensive? They're not too expensive for most groceries. You can automate some doors for well under a thousand dollars. Even low-budget independent living centers serving people with disabilities find a way to pay for them. Lorelee Stewart, who directs the Independent Living Center in Lynn, Massachusetts, tells us that, although her building landlord wouldn't pay for the automatic door opener they purchased, every other tenant in the building has found the door so useful that they have voluntarily agreed to share the minimal maintenance costs of the door!

When you do plan for an automatic door, apply the principles of universal design:

✔ Don't get a "special" door opener.

✔ Don't opt for a door that requires the user to push a "special" button to activate the door. Remember: anyone disabled enough to need an automatic door may also be too disabled to independently push such a button.

Don't make it special. Do what stores who buy the doors for the ease of their *regular* customers do: Get a mechanism that uses a light or other signal to automatically open the door.

A *Universal* Toilet Room

Ron Mace has a design he promotes for what he calls a "Universal Toilet Room." It's the ideal for new construction. It involves more than one accessible toilet stall — each one fitted a little bit differently — "because one toilet height is never going to be right for everyone." Accessibility standards currently call for a range of 17 to 19 inches.

The plan, says Mace, is to create a very large stall at the end of the restroom — all across the end. This one should have a regular toilet seat in it, 17 inches tall, which is still a standard height. This stall must be at least the 60-inch by 60-inch space we talked about, above.

Next to that, put in a stall that's 3 feet wide. In it put a toilet that's 19 inches tall. People who use walkers, have arthritis, bad backs or stiff joints and have trouble getting up and down from seats will find that toilet height easier. These folks often use canes and walkers or crutches, says Mace. The other stalls can be narrower and can have standard-height toilets. "That way you've got practically everyone covered," says Mace.

Mace's "Universal Toilet Room" design is close to what's required by the ADA Accessibility Guidelines in building new restrooms of 6 or more stalls. We suggest you use it in any restroom that has more than one stall.

It's well known among women that many of us routinely choose the larger, accessible stall in a public women's restroom — even though we have no disabilities. It's because they're roomier — they give us room to hang our coat without it falling into the toilet. They give us room to put down our briefcase, our parcels; to park our baby stroller alongside us. Bigger is definitely better.

Chapter 5
All About
Removing Structural Barriers

In Chapter 3,, we looked at things required by the law that don't require any structural changes — changes in attitude and changes in your policies and practices. Now it's time to look at removing what the law calls "architectural barriers" and "communication barriers that are structural in nature."

We will also try to give you a rough idea of what it might cost to do these things. Of course, costs vary widely. But in each case we've tried to let you know what it's cost at least in certain specific situations.

The figures we cite might surprise you. Do they seem low? If they do, consider this: A number of studies cited by Congresssional committees in debating the cost of this law showed that nearly 70 percent of accommodations cost under $500 per employee. If people with disabilities tell you anything, they will tell you that prices for simple access changes are often wildly inflated by builders or contrators nervous about building something a little diffferently.

Unfortunately, prices are also sometimes inflated by people out to make a buck because they've got you over a barrel. One example: Many contractors have sold companies "special" "handicap" sinks for restrooms. These "special" sinks could have been avoided altogether. Many people think that they must go to places like medical supply houses to purchase grab bars, when the local plumber's supply carries them for a fraction of the cost.

We have chosen standard prices from discount building supply stores for many of our quotes; and we've relied on do-it-yourselfers to take the high labor figures out of a lot of what are essentially one-day handyman projects. You can do this too, once you learn what's involved. In fact, you can do even better.

And if you're smart, you'll even be able to *cut these costs in half* — by using the new IRS Tax Credit we tell you about at the end of Chapter 7, "Remove Barriers & Increase Your Profits." Access changes that may add up to $4,000 in these pages might cost you well under $2,000. So read on.

When you alter your place (or build something new)

Any *alteration* you make to your place — and all *new construction* —must be accessible. "Potential patrons ... should be able to get to a store, get into the store and get to the areas where the goods are being provided" — this also includes making your employee lounges, cafeterias, exercise facilities, work stations and so on accessible, says the Department of Justice. New construction and alterations must comply with the ADA's Accessibility Guidelines. These Guidelines are similar to the access requirements many states already have in their building codes; in some cases they may go beyond them. State building departments are currently in the process of making sure state codes do not conflict with or are brought up to the requirements of this new federal law.

When you or your contractor applies for a building permit, the permit agency should mention these new standards. They come with the free Department of Justice rules that we have been encouraging you to order (See Appendix A). We suggest that you show a copy to the contractor who handles construction and alterations at your place.

One of the best things you can do is read the Accessibility Guidelines yourself. The technical language may seem daunting, but just having it on hand and looking it over casually will acquaint you much more readily with what you may ultimately be able to do in your place of public accommodation.

The Guidelines cover things like floor surfaces, parking and passenger loading zones, curb ramps, other ramps, entrances, stairs, elevators and wheelchair lifts, windows, doors, entrances, drinking fountains, restrooms and restroom fixtures including showers and bathing facilities as well as things like storage areas, alarms and warnings, telephones, assembly areas, built-in seating and tables as well as special sections on restaurants and cafeterias, shops, libraries, hotels and motels and transportation facilities.

Once you've read this chapter, the Guidelines may make more sense. Your goal is to give patrons "independent access."

Remember what Deborah McKeen said back at the start of Chapter 3: "I like the idea of being able to go in and out of a door without having to 'ask someone' first. Of course people will help you with it, but I am tired of having to ask. I don't want to have to ask. I want to go in and out and deal with other, more important issues in my day, like other people do."

"Readily-achievable" changes at your current place

Here are some examples of fairly easy things to do to remove barriers right now, without waiting until you plan any alterations or new construction. Many of these examples come from the Department of Justice's rules. As you can see, they're almost all "easily accomplishable." None of them are very difficult to do. Most of them can be done inexpensively.

Parking spots

Designate some close-in parking spaces as "accessible" by widening them and installing signs. People who need accessible parking spots need them at least 8 feet wide so they can unload their wheelchairs. Many people who use wheelchairs drive by themselves and don't have anyone to help them unload their chair; the need clear space for their van lift to lower or to swing their chair out from behind the driver's seat. Most codes and the Accessibility Guidelines call for one accessible space for every 25 spots in your lot, up to 100 spots, and then provide a chart to indicate the number required in larger lots.

If you're not altering your parking lot, you can simply restripe a few spots in your lot, making them wider. Install an official "access symbol" parking sign on a post in front of each spaces. Signs that cost from $6 to $15 are available in most hardware and building supply stores or by mail order from the suppliers in Appendix C.

Installing curb cuts and entry ramps

Can someone in a wheelchair actually get from the street or the accessible parking spots in your lot all the way to your door without unexpectedly running up against a step or curb?

That's happened to Mike Collins more than once. "The intersection I needed to cross had three curb cuts," he tells us. "Unfortunately, the corner I needed to get to was one that *didn't* have a curb cut."

"I just recently had to take my chair [Collins uses a motorized wheelchair] into the shop to replace the front axle, which I broke dropping over curbs that were supposed to have cuts in them — but didn't." That was over $200. Not having curb cuts where you need them is not only inconvenient, it's expensive for us — and dangerous. "I could have really been hurt," says Collins. "There's no excuse under the ADA not to put in curb cuts."

Would your wheelchair-riding customers run up against a curb, like Collins did? Find out. Ask someone who uses a chair to go over the route with you. Remember: no fair helping them get up low curbs! If they can't get in independently, then you need to add curb cuts and ramps.

Though it's better if a curb cut is made by cutting into the curb itself (a technology that every city works department has pretty much down pat by now — and you can call them for advice), a quick-and-dirty "curb ramp" can often do the trick, just by having a little asphalt poured. The trick is to make sure the asphalt is wide enough that a wheelchair can actually get up it without rolling off the side — and that it isn't so steep that you have to be a Hercules-in-a-wheelchair to push yourself up the incline.

Try it sometime: get in a wheelchair yourself and try to push up some of the ramps and curb cuts you find. It's a lot harder than you think. You have to remember: not everyone has strong arm muscles to compensate for an inability to walk. Not everyone has a motorized chair. Some people are elderly, being pushed by elderly spouses. Don't compromise and risk creating a ramp people can't use — or might get hurt on (risking costing you much more in possible legal costs later)!

The law says ramps, curb cuts and the like need "a slope of 1:12." That technical term means that for every inch of drop, your ramp should slope out 12 inches. If you're ramping an 8-inch curb, your ramp should ideally slope out about 8 feet to a nice, smooth finish that's flush with the parking lot or street. If you can't manage that, the law lets you "approximate" it under the "readily achievable" standard. Remember, what you're doing now isn't an *alteration* or *new construction.* You're simply doing what you can do, right now, to your present place, to make it as accessible as possible. If you were building a new wing with a new entrance, your contractor would have to follow the code to the letter. Lawmakers recognized that in the quick-and-dirty modifications required of you now, you might not be able to follow the code to the letter. But you should approximate it as much as possible.

Remember the Principle of The Most Disabled User, which we learned about in the last chapter: if it works for them, it will usually work for everyone! In this case, the "Most Disabled User" would be someone who hasn't the ability to push themselves easily — someone whom even a tiny, 1/2-inch lip at the curb's bottom would stop. Many disabled people do, in fact, fit this description. Ask somebody you know who's fairly small and not very athletic to get into a wheelchair and try to get up a curb ramp that has a "tiny" lip at the bottom. Don't be surprised to discover that they can't do it.

Your goal should be to make curb cuts and ramps *everyone* can use, easily and independently. The key is to show a "good faith effort," says Mace. "No reasonable person will fault you if you do this."

Quickly made wooden ramps out of 2 x 4s often work at curbs; you can build one for as little as $25 worth of lumber. Drive iron pegs into the ground to secure the wooden ramp from moving from the curb edge. Make sure the ramp has at least 3 feet of clear width for a wheelchair.

Ramps at entrances need a 5-foot by 5-foot square platform at the top so a person in a wheelchair doesn't roll back down trying to get the door open — unless you're building a ramp up to a porch that's at least this size.

Wooden ramps, less expensive than concrete ones, last many years if made from treated "deck" type lumber. Using the same construction techniques that do-it-yourselfers use to build backyard decks, many groups have built sturdy and attractive ramps. It shouldn't cost a do-it-yourselfer more than a couple of hundred dollars to build a standard ramp and platform to span one to three steps at an entrance: a 5-foot by 5-foot wooden deck attached to a 8- to 10-foot ramp, at least 3 feet wide, with wooden handrails. Your local independent living center (Appendix B) should be able to refer you to somebody who does this kind of work.

Although portable ramps do exist on the market, nobody encourages their use as a way to make your place accessible. They're often flimsy and unstable and prone to being removed so that they're not always available to disabled people when they need them.

Fixing Difficult Surfaces

The Department of Justice suggests "removing high-pile carpeting, low-density carpeting, plush carpeting." These types of floor coverings make it very difficult for people in wheelchairs and people who have trouble walking already. Tightly woven indoor-outdoor carpeting is not only less expensive to install than plush carpeting; it works better for everyone — not to mention people pushing movable files or delivering office supplies or the mail with pushcarts. Nonslip surfaces are important as well. If your floors are marble or some other highly slippery surface, think about installing some nonslip material to provide a "path of travel." If you aren't able yet to replace your carpeting, think of removing it at least in the "path of travel."

"Path of travel" is a term used in the rules. It means "a continuous, unobstructed way of pedestrian passage" to other areas. A "path of travel" to your restroom would mean the path a person must take to get to and back from the restroom, including everything from the sidewalk up to your entrance, including the "path" to and back from the restroom. It would include your elevator if the restroom is on another floor from your accessible entrance. We'll talk more about "paths of travel" when we discuss alterations, later on.

Getting into the building

Now that we're up to the entrance, can we get in?

Can deaf people get into my building? Does this seem like a trick question? It isn't. Many small businesses operate in large office complexes, some of which require a visitor to call in on a phone security system in the lobby. If you're deaf, how can you do that? How can you hear the buzzer that buzzes you in?

This is one of a number of thorny problems still being resolved by those who worked hard on putting this law in place. If your place is in such a building, it would be wise to call one of the sources listed in Appendix C and ask for advice.

If visitors routinely use such a security system, is it low enough for someone in a wheechair to reach? Are there braille markings on the door to alert a blind person that she must use the security phone to gain entrance?

Making doorways accessible

In order for a wheelchair to get through a door, most wheelchair users need a minimum clear opening of 32 inches when the door is open 90 degrees. That's what the ADA's Accessibility Guidelines require. Many entrances into today's new buildings are already wide enough. But doors to dressing rooms, restrooms, customer service areas and other areas inside your building may not be. If any of your doors are narrower than 32 inches when open, you should consider widening them as the next step you take after building a ramp. An interior door that it isn't in a load-bearing wall should be able to be widened easily by following one of the many do-it-yourself guides available from home supply centers. A doorframe should be able to be widened and a new door purchased for a couple of hundred dollars at the most. Of couse you can pay much more, too — depending on how expensive your labor is and what style of door you purchase.

We, along with most people with disabilities, will urge you to use inexpensive methods of making changes. More expensive methods aren't necessary. Besides, if you claim you can't make a change because it's too expensive, and a disabled person shows you a way that's "readily achievable" (without too much difficulty or expense) to do it, and you refuse to, you may be liable under the law. So it's to your benefit to try inexpensive ways to make changes.

When a doorway is only an inch or so too narrow, replacing the door's hinges with "offset hinges" can often solve the problem. These hinges (common brands are Stanley Swing Clear hinges or Ply Gems, available at larger building supply stores) allow the door to swing entirely out of the doorway, increasing manuevering room to the full width of the door frame. Sets of offset hinges should cost under $50 and are installed much like normal door hinges.

An extremely simple solution for the inaccessibility caused by revolving doors is simply to keep the adjoining "regular" doors unlocked and indicate that patrons may also enter through the regular door.

Requiring patrons to use a revolving door (and keeping other entrances locked, as is sometimes done) is now illegal.

Many entrance doors are extremely heavy. They cause problems for people who aren't even disabled. The law requires doors that need no more than 5 pounds of force to open. Many of these doors can be "lightened" by turning a screw in the opening/closing mechanism at the top of the door. It costs no money at all to do this.

Replace any round doorknobs with lever handles. These handles are often available for under $10 at discount building-supply stores. If your doors don't require turning handles to open them, lessening the amount of force required to open them may be sufficient. Ask a disabled person who has limited hand dexterity, like a quadriplegic, to show you the kinds of doors that are most easily opened. Doors that swing both ways and can be opened by the push of a wheelchair are probably best.

Unlocking, Lowering, Rearranging, Repositioning

How often are patrons blocked from moving around a store by temporary displays that close off their passage? How often does someone in a chair go to a restaurant restroom only to discover their path to the otherwise-accessible restroom blocked by a cigarette vending machine sticking out into the hallway? This happens more than one wheelchair user wants to think about, she says. "We had a brand new restaurant open — lots of advertising, good reviews. It was completely accessible, too. I couldn't wait to go.

"That was just what happened in the restaurant, too," she said. "I couldn't wait to 'go.' I figured the restrooms were accessible, so I didn't restrict myself as I usually do; I ordered extra drinks. That was a mistake. When I went to the restroom after the meal, I found I couldn't get in. A big cigarette machine stuck out nearly 2 feet into the 4-foot hallway, and a restroom that I should have been able to use became off-limits to me."

Do you have turnstiles that let patrons into your shopping area or sports arena? Eliminating them is the best thing you can do to increase space for people in wheelchairs to enter the same way as everyone else. Until you remodel or rebuild, simply arranging things to create an entry passage 3 feet wide will work well as a temporary solution. Remember to clearly mark it with a sign using the wheelchair symbol so someone entering your store, stadium, theater, etc. for the first time can independently see how she's to get in without having to ask about a "special handicap entrance."

In many stores, Deborah McKeen finds it hard, she says, to be "sitting down below the counter and waiting interminably for someone to notice me." "If you have a whole row of 4-foot high counters," says Marian Schooling Vessels, who uses a wheelchair, "how about lowering some of them — so you can see me when I come in?" Lowering cashiers' counters not only helps people in wheelchairs. It helps children, short people and people carrying lots of items. It's easier to load up a counter with purchases if the counter's at waist level.

It shouldn't be hard to rearrange tables, chairs, vending machines, display racks and other furniture to allow passage for people in wheelchairs or using walkers to move about easily. Before you do, though, please have several people in wheelchairs come to your location (after you've built your ramp and they can get in!) to make suggestions. Sometimes things that seem logical to you have a flaw that someone who is in a wheelchair can spot immediately. The access standards call for aisles of 3 feet; you need an area 5 feet by 5 feet for two chairs to pass. If your aisles are long, as in a grocery store, you may need some of these 5-foot square open areas to allow for "turn around." This can often be accomplished by re-thinking your temporary display areas and consolidating them. We can't stress too much the need to have a group of potential customers in wheelchairs visit your location to scope it out and give you pointers.

Some people in wheelchairs can reach as high as 50 or so inches by turning sideways; however, most of us can't reach nearly that high. Reposition goods on your shelves so that a range of the items you sell is available to us at wheelchair level — somewhere between 35 and 42 inches. One way to do this is to use top, middle and lower shelves to display the same items. For example: if you run an office supply store, don't put all the boxes of manila folders on top shelves, the boxes of legal pads on middle shelves and boxes of envelopes on lower shelves; use the same shelves to make a vertical display of the same item all the way up and down. It's also wise to display signs prominently telling customers to "ask store personnel for help with items you cannot reach."

Once you decide on your new accessible layout, don't keep changing things. Blind people can move about independently once they know where things are. Blind patrons of your place need to feel comfortable in finding things where they can expect them. Once they walk through your store with a sighted store clerk and learn where products are kept, where the vending machines are, where sales items can be found, they can be expected to find these places independently on subequent visits — unless everything has been rearranged.

Blind people can't see things that stick out from the wall, like signs, wall-mounted phones and other objects and could bump into them if they stick out more than about 4 inches, unless there's something beneath the "protruding object" to warn a blind person who's using a cane to navigate.

A meeting with blind advocates should be a must for you. They can show you how to decide on locations for things that make it easier for them to navigate and how to handle things like protruding objects.

We haven't listed costs for this section because most of the things we discuss are not new purchases; they require moving things and re-arranging things. Usually, these are tasks that can be performed by you or your staff, and cost can be negligible.

Making your public phone accessible

Ask the phone company to come in and reposition at least one of your phones so that someone in a wheelchair can reach the coin slot. The coin slot should be no higher than 48 inches; lower is better. If it's the only phone the public uses, attaching a small, 4- to 6-inch shelf-like bench at one side might be helpful for tall people. Whatever you do, though, don't put a bench where it blocks the access of a wheelchair user! Remember the Principle of the Most Disabled User: While someone in a wheelchair can't stand up to reach a phone that's too high, even a tall person can bend down for a minute or two to dial.

While you're at it, ask the phone company about installing an amplified receiver. They're a standard option for today's pay phones.

Equip your phone area with a bright light to help people with low vision to read phone numbers and take notes. This, of course, can help *everyone*. Provide a TDD machine for deaf people (see our next chapter). Simple TDDs can cost less than $200. A list of manufacturers' toll-free numbers is listed in Appendix C. Or ask your local disability group where to buy one. If you don't want to attach the TDD machine to the phone, post a conspicuous sign: TDD available at cashier's (at check out; at Customer Service, etc.) When you renovate or add new phones, you must comply with the Accessibility Guidelines; there are specific requirements about TDDs and amplified receivers.

Elevators

Adding an elevator? If so; it should be accessible — a disabled person using a wheelchair should be able to fit into it; the panel should be low enough for them to reach it; elevator buttons should have raised/braille markings (these are pretty standard in new elevator control panels today). Residential elevators are available for around $5,000, says Dianne Piastro.

If you already have an elevator, add raised and braille markings on elevator control buttons. You can buy sets of them from dealers in Appendix C for about $4 apiece; or your elevator service company can provide and install them (this usually costs more, unless your service contract covers it already). New elevators are now required by law to be accessible; the elevator buttons lower and braille/raised signage. If your elevator's buttons are too high to reach from a wheelchair, think of doing what Richard Dodds (of Region 2's Disability and Business Technical Assistance Center) once did: his group made a telescoping pole out of an old tripod to be used by people who couldn't reach the buttons! Would something like this work for you? Call the Region 2 Center (Appendix B) if you want to discuss this option. Your local independent living center may have come up with clever solutions, too. Check with them.

Lights and signs

Many of us with low vision or who are losing vision as we age find things much easier to see and read with bright light. Poorlyilluminated signs in dimly-lit foyers cause us real problems. These kinds of problems can be easily and inexpensively solved by increasing the wattage of lighting at signs, or installing lights where people must read directories or other signs. Glare makes reading difficult, too. Check to make sure the light illuminates signs brightly, and that protective glass doesn't create a glare that makes it hard to see through.

Increasing the size of the lettering in your directory can often help, too. This can be done easily and quickly by simply purchasing larger size type from your display company. The companies in Appendix C provide braille lettering too; you can install it next to or below a variety of signs for pennies a word.

Clearly readable signs can also make your place inviting to people who depend almost entirely on visual information — deaf and hard-of-hearing patrons. Think about providing signs to eliminate having to have people ask where things are — which would require them having to understand your response, too. An afternoon going through your place with members of an organization of Deaf people (with an interpreter they select and you pay for) can give you many ideas as to how to make your place visually clear. When you do install new signs, remember to use lettering big enough, and with bright enough lighting, that people with low vision can read it comfortably.

Installing braille signs/prices next to items is an added bonus you may want to provide, too to come close to providing *universal* access. (See "Adding braille signs," page 78.)

The ADA Accessibility Guidelines call for lettering that's three inches high on most signs, such as signs next to doors, room numbers, etc. Signs should be installed at about five feet off the ground. Braille signage can be put under or next to them. Appendix C lists sources for braille signs and raised pictorial symbols that comply with the law; these items are inexpensive, ranging from a few cents per letter to $6 for specific signs and symbols.

A word to the wise, though, about braille signs: often it's better to have a company familiar with working in braille prepare phrases for you — which they will do for a reasonable cost, than trying to write out a phrase like "please contact sales desk" letter for letter. This is because braille uses a number of contractions and shortcuts that you are likely not familiar with; spelling these phrases out letter for letter in "braille" may result in you writing something you didn't really intend to say! Get advice on this from a blind person who knows braille; or contact one of the companies in the Appendix C that make braille signs and ask for advice.

Is your seating 'integrated?'

If your place has a theater, screening room, conference room or other place where an audience sits, you can no longer restrict people in wheelchairs to one section apart from their friends. Theater-goers who use wheelchairs, says the Department of Justice, have "historically been relegated to inferior seating in the back of assembly areas" and separated from "family and friends. . . . People in wheelchairs should have the same opportunity to enjoy movies, plays and similar events with their families and friends, just as other patrons do." Either take out some of your seats to let disabled people sit at ends of regular rows, or provide portable chairs so people can sit next to their friends in wheelchairs.

Water fountains

Is your water fountain able to be used by someone sitting in a wheelchair? Does it stick out from the wall, and, if it does, have you checked with a blind consultant about the best way to let blind people be aware of its presence? If you put in a new water fountain, it will have to be done in compliance with the codes. For now, why not install a paper cup dispenser within easy reach of someone in a wheelchair — so that the "business end" of the dispenser is between 36 and 42 inches from the floor. With this, they can get a cup and get water from your inaccessible water fountain. Or they may choose to take the cup into the restroom and get water from the sink faucet — if you've made sure the sink is one they can get up under, and the handles are lever-type. Cost? About $3 from your grocery or discount store for a paper cup dispenser and cups.

Making your restrooms accessible

Many people who must rely on wheelchairs for mobility simply stay home because, even if we can get into a restaurant or a theater, we know the restroom isn't accessible. And having to "hold it" isn't a fun proposition for any of us, disabled or non-disabled. Making your place's restroom accessible is one of the best things you can do to increase the patronage of people with serious mobility problems.

Tragically, many of today's restrooms that purport to be "accessible" remain impossible for people in wheelchairs to use. There are many reasons for this. Sometimes it's because the builder simply has not followed the state codes or "skimped." The principle of "Almost Isn't Good Enough" is nowhere truer than in in a restroom that is *almost* — but not truly — big enough to use. Or not big enough to use in privacy.

Marilyn Phillips has a name for these kinds of restrooms. She calls them "Houdini Accessible Restrooms:" "You have to be Houdini to use them." These restrooms are "accessible" only if the door remains open. "How embarrassing!" says Phillips. "People who aren't disabled don't have to pee with everyone else watching!" Or they're "accessible" only if a friend comes in to manually turn her chair around. In Maryland, which already has access laws, Phillips has filed complaints against Houdini Accessible restrooms — and won.

How can you avoid Houdini Access?

Make sure they're big enough. Big is almost always the key. If you have three toilet stalls in your restrooms, don't just push the partition of one over a little. The "minimum" 36 inches by 48 inches that the ADA's Accessibility Guidelines say are "enough" for a wheelchair are only "enough" if you have enough other room to manuever in. A much better solution is to turn two stalls into one by removing one toilet entirely and taking out one partition. It's a much easier, simple and cheaper solution — in existing restrooms, anyway. Try to make sure there's the 5-foot by 5-foot space inside the toilet partition, after the door is locked and in addition to the space the toilet takes up.

Sometimes the best way to get enough space is to remove toilet partitions entirely and, by putting a lock on the restroom door itself, turning what was formerly a 2- or 3-person restroom into a private restroom. This is preferable to withholding access entirely. If your men's room and women's room adjoin, turn them into one "family" restroom with a lock and a single toilet inside.

Privacy. Don't forget to install a lock on the accessible toilet stall — one that works. Those of us in wheelchairs deserve as much privacy as nondisabled patrons. If you don't have separate stalls but merely a toilet room, make sure the lock on the restroom door itself is able to be worked by the most severely disabled patron.

Your locks should be ones that can be turned easily by someone with limited fingering ability. Ask your disability advisor about this, or visit a building supply store and look at their array of locks. Sometimes the simplest thing — an old fashioned, large hook-and-eye lock that can be manipulated even by someone using only their fist — works best. An even simpler bar and slot lock might work better. Try it yourself. If you had no finger movement — only a fist — could you work this lock? Try it.

Do I need a new "special" toilet? Ron Mace points out that there's no sure way to know which height toilet seat works best for all patrons. If providing the "Universal Toilet Room" Mace suggests in the previous chapter is beyond your present budget or abilities, don't worry about installing a new toilet. Manufacturers sell "seat risers" that can be installed on toilets to raise the seat height. Check with your Regional Center or a local group of people who need them, like an arthritis support group, to see what they advise. Much more important are installing grab bars.

Grab bars. These are available from plumbing supply stores for under $25. They come in a variety of lengths. The 32-inch ones, 3/4-inch in diameter, can be mounted easily by screwing them into the studs behind your wall (most walls are built with studs spaced every 16 inches). If you buy 24-inch long grab bars, you have to reinforce the wall in order to secure them. The ADA's Accessibility Guidelines tell you to install grab bars 36 inches up from the floor. It's a big help to install them on either side and behind the toilet — because different people need them in different places. (You can't have too many grab bars, we say!)

Other things for toilet stalls. Simple things are sometimes overlooked. Is the toilet paper dispenser within easy reach of someone on the toilet who can't move his arms very well? (It's not going to do any good if it's even two inches out of reach, is it?) Does the grab bar now obstruct it? If so, move it. In deciding on precise locations of things like these, it's invaluable to bring in a wheelchair user who has advised other people on this kind of thing. Then you can see why certain things work; and things become clear to you. As always: remember the Principle of the Most Disabled User that we discussed in the previous chapter. *Make it so everyone can use it.*

Fixing your sink. If you have a vanity sink in your restroom, people in wheelchairs can't get up to the sink easily. Remove the vanity but leave the sink. That's not hard to do; it would probably take a carpenter an hour or so. An even simpler solution is to leave the vanity but remove the doors, providing at least some "pull-up" space under the counter.

People who are paralyzed often have no feeling in their legs. Insulate water pipes under your sink with insulation wrapping available at building supply stores to protect against burns.

Get rid of those round faucets and replace them with lever faucets or a single-action lever faucet! These can often be found for under $25 on sale at discount plumbing supply stores and come with do-it-yourself installation instructions. You needn't equip all your sinks with these (though it would be nice.) They take a klutz about a half-hour to install. If you're handy with a screwdriver they'll take even less time.

Reposition the soap dispenser so someone in a wheelchair can use it — without having to reach so far or so high that the handful of soap drips down their arm! Check the thermostat on the hot-water tank so that there's no chance of someone scalding themselves. Even with lever faucets, some people have limited dexterity and cannot easily control water flow or temperature. Reposition the towel dispenser down to about 38 inches off the floor. Or place a stack of disposable towels on the counter in easy reach. Move the tampon dispenser down also.

Make sure the tampon dispenser, paper towel rack and soap dispenser aren't above a trash can or something else that blocks access.

Install a full-length mirror. These can be purchased for under $10 at discount stores and take about 10 minutes to put up. Don't put the trash can, a chair or anything else that obstructs view in front of it.

If the light switch isn't within wheelchair-user reach, turn it on and tape over it so a walking person doesn't turn it off, leaving a wheelchair user unable to turn it on by themselves.

Put the trash can in an out-of-the-way place. And once you decide that's where it belongs, leave it there. Blind people who frequent your establishment are helped when things stay in their assigned spaces and can be anticipated to be where they were the last time they visited.

Make sure the restroom signs are clearly understandable. Avoid "cute" names like "Does" and "Bucks" or "Guys" and "Dolls" that are confusing to people with mental limitations (or people learning English!). The best signs are the pictorial symbols available at sign suppliers. Install raised and braille restroom signage, too (see "Adding braille signs," below.)

Making alarm systems work for deaf or blind patrons

Emergency alarms in new and altered construction will be required by the new law to give both visual and audible warnings. There are alarm systems on the market that do this; your system, depending on its "class," may already have both. If it doesn't, check with the contractor who installed your system to see if you can get both. Soon your alarm supplier will probably advise you of "upgrades" available because of the new law.

Because of the complicated and regulated nature of alarm systems, we don't feel we can give you a typical cost for this. Some places, such as a home office, are required to have only a simple emergency system such as a smoke detector. Public theaters, restaurants and other places must have elaborate systems. Our best advice: check with your alarm system installer.

Adding braille signs

Not all blind people read braille. But many do. "The next generation of blind people is starting to advocate strongly for the use of braille," says Bonnie O'Day. We may see a resurgence of braille as it becomes easier for blind people to produce and get documents in braille because of the advent of low-cost home computer braille printers.

Braille signage is inexpensive enough for you to add braille signs to restroom doors, elevator floors and office numbers.

Think about making braille signs for signs you post for the public, such as your check cashing policy.

Both standard words ("Men," "Women," "Office," etc.) and individual braille letters with which you can compose your own words are available from several national mail-order sign distributors listed in Appendix C. These companies have catalogs with many standard signs in both lettering and braille; they will also make signs to your own wording. Prices range from a few cents to $4 for standard signs. Custom work costs more.

About alterations and new construction

Remember: The law distinguishes between things that you can do right now, that are considered "readily achievable," to create access, even if you aren't yet making structural alterations or doing any new construction, and actual alterations and new construction.

When you do alter something or build something new, it *has to be accessible.* In new construction, access rarely costs more than 1 percent — if anything — more. This has been proven over and over again as builders have started to build more and more things with access, some of them using *universal* design principles, or following requirements in many state building codes.

Gregory Solas points out that state building code departments can provide you with much advice about complying with accessibility guidelines. And, he reminds us, they provide the advice for *free.* Giving your state code enforcement division a call might be a good idea. Remember, of course, that they are busy, and will be even busier now that this new law is in effect. Try to have succinct questions for them.

The federal law says that whenever you alter a structural element, like moving an electrical outlet, the altered one has to comply with the law's accessibility guidelines. It also says that when you alter any area that "affects or could affect the usability of or access to an area" that contains a "primary function" (that is, a "major activity for which the facility is intended"), then the "path of travel" to that area also has to be made accessible. If things like restrooms or telephones are along that "path of travel," they, too, have to be made accessible along with the alteration — unless, says the law, the "cost and scope" of doing that is what the rules call "disproportionate to the cost of the overall alteration."

Things like remodeling merchandise display areas or employee work areas in a department store, installing a computer center in an accounting firm or replacing an inaccessible floor surface in the customer service area of a bank are some examples the Department of Justice offers to give you an idea of what's considered an alteration to a place that's considered a "primary function."

Here's another example. If you decide to take an unused back room of your home office and turn it into training room for clients of your home computer consulting business — then clients have to be able to get from the front room to the back room, and if there's a restroom along the hallway that clients are allowed to use, then you have to make it accessible too.

This chapter has showed you things that can be done right now — "readily achievable" ways to provide access. Whenever you change or add anything, always try to make it accessible in a way that all disabled people can use it — following the principles of *universal* design we discussed in our previous chapter. We strongly encourage you to get a copy of the ADA Accessibility Guidelines and use them — even if you're simply making "readily achievable" changes that don't, by law, have to adhere to the guidelines. You'll be making your place truly accessible, and you'll be saving dollars in the long run.

The ADA reminds us that not only must we remove barriers, we have an obligation to make sure the accessible features of our place continue to work. Accessible toilet stalls that do not close and lock properly must be fixed promptly; doors that become heavier must be lightened; braille markings that are vandalized must be replaced.

In addition to making the kinds of "readily achievable" changes discussed in this chapter, you may also need to have things like TDDs and interpreters for deaf people, things like braille or large print programs and menus for blind people. These are called "auxiliary aids and services" under the law. They're discussed in our next chapter.

Chapter 6
All About
Auxiliary Aids and Services

Deaf people have known constant discrimination because those of us who can hear simply assumed that Deaf people, because they could not hear, were somehow "less" than we were. The term "deaf and dumb" is a reminder of that era; it is a term Deaf people hate — and justly so. "There's a perception that your intelligence goes down in relation to the severity of your disability," says Jo Waldron, President of Phoenix Management, Inc., who, being deaf, tells the common story of having a companion being asked "what does *she* want" to eat at a restaurant, rather than asking her.

Blind people have faced discrimination, too. Bonnie O'Day recalled for us in an earlier chapter that a teacher for whom she applied to be an assistant told her flatly that putting her notes onto cassette tape, so O'Day could type them up in her job as teaching assistant, was simply "not the way I do things." Don Galloway, of Washington, D.C. was recently denied a spot on a jury — a clearly illegal move forbidden under the Rehabilitation Act — simply because he was blind.

Stan Greenberg tells us that the discrimination blind people face comes from the same place all discrimination comes from: ignorance or prejudice. "People think we are incapable; that anything we do needs incredible support from someone who's not disabled. We can't possibly do anything independently, people think; anything we do independently is viewed as kind of a miracle that the average person with a disability is incapable of." Here are some of the kinds of remarks Greenberg says he's heard: "How amazing! You use a computer that *talks*!" "But who's going to correct your typing errors?" "What happens if you walk into the water cooler and knock it over?" "All of that," says Greenberg, "stems from ignorance."

As both Weiner's and O'Day's stories should tell us, deaf people and blind people face discrimination often because of non-disabled people's refusal to switch from the "standard" methods over to new methods of communicating that include people with disabilities.

In today's technological age, there's little excuse for unwillingness to accommodate people who can't see well, can't hear well or who may not understand well what they do hear and see. Under the law, you must use "auxiliary aids and services" to communicate with them. This chapter explains some simple ways to begin to do that.

The law requires you to "take steps ... to ensure" that no one with a disability is "excluded, denied services, segregated or otherwise treated differently" than others simply because of "an absence of auxiliary aids and services." Thus, according to the law, you have to make sure that no one with a disability is excluded, denied services, segregated or treated differently from your other patrons. You have to provide the "auxiliary aid" or "service" that's needed so that they aren't excluded or segregated. These may indeed cost money — for interpreters, for readers, for braille and large print. Don't forget, though, over half your ongoing expenditures may be able to be reclaimed as a tax credit. (See the end of our next chapter to learn how you can claim the tax credit.)

Communicating with Deaf and hard-of-hearing people

"I worked as a carpenter in California," says Steve Weiner, who's deaf. "I could read blueprints; my crew boss could not. And I wanted a promotion. But I was denied one because I couldn't use the phone. That was almost 20 years ago. My dad, who's also deaf, was denied a promotion for all 35 years of his working life because he could not use the phone," Weiner continues, now talking over the phone to us via a "telephone device for the deaf" (called a TDD). He trained several people who eventually became his bosses, or executives in the company. And when the company merged, they let him go, because he couldn't use the phone!"

We rarely think of how significant the telephone is to modern life. Deaf people have been isolated from using the phone to communicate, which is ironic in view of the fact that the inventor of the phone, Alexander Graham Bell, invented it almost as a "mistake" while trying to create a device to enable him to commuicate with deaf people!

TDDs?

Before people ever come to your place of public accommodation, they often call you. And it's actually extremely easy to communicate with deaf people over the phone today — provided you have a "telecommunications device for the deaf," or TDD, to use. Though TDDs are as standard today among people who are part of the Deaf culture as phones are in the hearing culture, the problem remains one of "us" and "them": few hearing people own a TDD. And that's really a shame. For without two TDDs, no communication can take place.

TDDs are pretty simple. They're about the size of a very small laptop computer, which is pretty much what they are. They have a keyboard, like a typewriter, and either a place to hook a phone line into, like a phone has, or a "cradle" into which you can place the headset of a standard phone — or both. They cost anywhere from just under $200 for a very basic model to several hundred dollars. Like phones, some TDDs are set up to work with answering machines; some have repeat dialing and number memory. Some have printout capabilities, to print out the phone conversation like a printing calculator does.

Similar but not the same as faxes and computer modems, the signal TDDs send over the phone wires can communicate only with another TDD — not a fax or a computer (you can buy a computer chip that can turn a standard modem into a TDD, however.)

Or the relay service?

In many states today, though, you can talk with a TDD user without having a TDD yourself: through what's called a "deaf relay service." The Americans with Disabilities Act requires a nationwide relay service to be in effect by 1993. Over 30 states have relay service in use. *To find out if your state has one, call your phone company today!*

To use a relay service, you dial your state's toll-free 800 number. You'll be connected to an operator who will ask if you're a first-time user, and, if so, will explain how the service works (if they don't, you should ask, if it's your first time to use a relay service). Basically, the operator calls the deaf party — you provide the number and tell them who you're trying to reach — and translates over a TDD your voice message. You need to speak to the operator slowly enough to allow him to type; there will be a few seconds' pause while the party you're calling types in a response and your operator reads it to you. You must also remember that the operator is strictly a *relay*. You are not talking to the operator; you are talking directly to the deaf person who is calling you. So don't say things like, "tell her my store opens at 9 am." Simply say, "my store opens at 9 am." Remember, you are talking directly to the deaf person. The operator is only a relay.

Though the call to the relay service is a toll-free call, the call to the deaf party is billed as any regular call.. If it's a long distance call, that long-distance charge will show up on your bill as though you had made the TDD call yourself.

So: do I need a TDD?

Though nationwide relay service will be operational by mid-1993, you may still need a TDD on your premises. If customers of your "place of public accommodation" have access to a public phone as part of your services, then you have to make a TDD available to them as part of that phone service which you provide all customers routinely.

You may choose to provide a TDD next to your public phone, or you may wish to keep it at a cashier's desk or other easily accessible place. If you do that, you need to remember to have a sign at the public phone indicating where the deaf caller can get the TDD. You can't charge extra for letting a customer use the TDD.

Places like hotels and motels will have to have TDDs available for deaf guests in their rooms; there will also need to be one at the front desk or switchboard so deaf hotel guests can use it to order room service, inquire about checkout time, etc. Remember: the purpose of the law is to ensure that people with hearing impairments can make use of the same services everybody else does. Banks, too, will need TDDs that enable deaf customers to call in via TDD and check their account balances via phone, just as hearing customers do now. Many institutions today use automated phone systems to allow callers to check things like account balances, transfer funds or inquire about billing; these services can't be accessed through the relay service, says Sy Dubow of the ADA Communications Accommodation Project. Such institutions will have to make these services accessible via TDD to TDD-using customers. If you need more information on how this is being done, Dubow's project (Appendix B) may be able to help.

Using a TDD

It's simple: instead of talking, you type back and forth. What you've typed can be read on a mini-screen; but it's all done in real-time: what you type is going over the line as you type it. TDDs are easy to use and come with instructions. There's an etiquette to TDD use: To signal you're finished with what you're saying, and ready for the other party to respond, you type, GA (for "go ahead"). The person on the other end will do the same. When you're ready to hang up, you type "GA SK." To signal that they, too, are hanging up, the party on the other end will type, "SK SK."

When you're called by someone using a TDD, you'll hear a signal much like a fax or computer modem signal when you pick up the phone. When that happens, switch over to your TDD and use it.

TDDs have been one of the pieces of technology that have made deaf people able to compete with hearing people on an equal basis. Weiner says that when Maryland's TDD relay service finally began at the end of 1992, he made over 25 calls in a couple of days.

Communicating with deaf patrons in face-to-face, one-on-one situations

Once a deaf person arrives at your place of public accommodation, can they even get in the door? Maybe not — if your office is in a building that uses a phone-security system to let people in. How can a deaf person talk on that phone? If you have such a system, contact one of the sources in Appendix B or C to discuss the problem, which is still being worked out.

Once through your front door, a deaf or hard-of-hearing customer faces another door that must be opened: the door of communication. How should you communicate with deaf patrons in person? Do you use written notes? An interpreter? Lipreading? Do you shout?

All through his years in school, from grade school through college, says Frank Bowe, "I never had an interpreter in any course I took. I had teachers who gave tests orally, by reading the questions aloud in class. I was lucky if I understood a few of the questions, let alone all of them." Today, says Bowe, "We'd call this discrimination. But at the time I didn't realize that I had any rights."

Should we provide interpreters?

"Most people who are deaf or hard-of-hearing," says Frank

Bowe, "do not use American Sign Language. That's because they lost their hearing later in life." Most early-deafened indviduals, he says, "know at least some signs and fingerspelling. It's a cultural thing," he adds. "If you grow up with a hearing loss, you tend to accept it and adjust to it" — so you learn signing. "On the other hand, if you grow up hearing, you tend to resist acknowledging the loss, along with everything that comes with that loss: the need for hearing aids, for lipreading, for sign language. You try to get by as you always have."

On the other hand, some people born deaf may have almost no knowlege of English. American Sign Language may be their native language. Or they may have no true language at all. They may have never communicated except with the most rudimentary signs.

American Sign Language (ASL) is a true language just as are the spoken and written languages we are more familiar with. It is a visual, manual language. It requires skill to learn, as does any language. "Signed English" is a kind of manual transliteration of the English language into manual signs. It is not the same as ASL, and, many culturally Deaf people would maintain it is therefore not as complete for them as ASL. There is also "fingerspelling," which, as its name implies, is the literal translation, letter by letter, of English (or other language) words into the letters of the manual alphabet. Fingerspelling is used in fluent interpretation to translate words such as proper names, product names, specific terms, etc.

You can't tell by looking whether a deaf person who comes to your place uses ASL or not. You need to ask. A key rule of the ADA is that you must provide the "aid or service" that works for that *person*. How do you ask, you say, if you don't know sign language? What about writing to the deaf person on a pad of paper?

For small shopkeepers to communicate brief items, that might work OK, says Steve Weiner. It depends on the level of communication. The name of a product, a price, writing down an address — that kind of simple communication can work with a pad and paper. If you run a small diner, for example, and all the items you serve are on the menu, deaf customers may be able to communicate quite adequately by pointing to a menu item. If you own a hardware store, deaf customers may be able to find what they need easily by the clear layout and display of items, buttressed by a store catalog which you can hand them to show you the item they're seeking. More complicated or serious communication, though, may need an interpreter.

The law specifies that you must provide a "qualified interpreters." Generally, that means someone whose training qualifies them to interpret for deaf people in a variety of situations and who does this professionally. Too often people who know a few fingerspellings, or a friend or relative of a deaf person, has been pressed into service to double as interpreter.

There are many reasons why this is a bad practice. Aside from the simple fact that a deaf patron deserves more skilled interpreting ability than such people often have, it is often unethical, as we mentioned earlier, to involve people with personal connections in discussions of a legal, medical or private nature.

If you have someone on your staff or in your office who has some experience in signing, they may be of service for simple, initial interpreting, things like communicating basics, things about office hours, prices, and so on — or to communicate to you specifics about the deaf client's request for a more qualified interpreter, for instance!

If you have someone available who can do this rough-and-ready interpreting, it's a service to deaf clients to post a conspicuous "ASK FOR SIGN LANGUAGE INTERPRETER, IF NEEDED" sign near your entrance so a deaf patron will know, upon entering, that they can ask at least some basic questions in Sign and expect to get answers.

This is the kind of thing that costs you no extra money but goes a long way toward building good will and helping business relations.

How would interpreting work in my store or business?

If you are an attorney, a doctor, a psychotherapist, an accountant, an insurance office or an undertaker, you may someday get a call, via your state's telephone relay service, placed on a TDD by a deaf person. They may want your services.

One of the first things you should ask them, when setting up an appointment for them to come into your office, is "do you need an interpreter?" This is easy if done via TDD. If in person, pen and paper may suffice. Discuss with the potential client what they need in terms of an interpreter. If they say they need an interpreter, it's your job to provide it. You may wish to ask for recommendations from your client, who likely knows interpreters. Before receiving that first call, a smart business owner or professional has contacted their local interpreters' registry (See Appendix C) to line up potential interpreters to hire. Ask your local independent living center, which has had experience hiring intepreters themselves, how best to go about this.

"I certainly ask for an in interpreter when I go to the doctor," Steve Weiner tells us. "It's my body; it's my health." Weiner tells the story of a former executive director of the National Association of the Deaf, "who died young because of poor communication with his doctor. So I will certainly demand an interpreter," says Weiner.

When an interpreter interprets, you need to remember that it's you and the deaf person who are having the conversation — not you and the interpreter. (Watch on TV news the way interpreters work when foreign dignitaries meet with the President for pointers).

Jo Waldron reminds us that it's important to remember that the sign language interpreter and the deaf person must be able to see each other — a commonsense enough point but one which is often forgotten. In a one-on-one situation, the hearing person and the interpreter should both face the deaf person.

Sometimes the simplest points of etiquette are forgotten by the hearing person, due to unfamiliarity or nervousness. Remember: you are talking to the deaf person. The interpreter is not part of the conversation. When talking, say, "you" — not "he" or "she." Try to talk slowly enough to allow the interpreter to interpret clearly. The interpreter may ask you to spell proper names or technical terms; try to remember if you're asked.

What if an interpreter costs too much?

Can you conclude that providing an interpreter costs too much and therefore is an "undue burden?" (The law says you don't have to provide accommodations like these if to do so is an "undue burden.") Yes, you can; but anyone who decides to tell a client they can't have an interpreter risks having that client sue them. And, as Sy Dubow of the ADA Communications Accommodation Project (See Appendix B) points out, you'd have to prove that the cost of providing a $30 interpreter is an "undue burden" based on your "overall financial resources." A court would have to look at things like your annual salary. If you're an accountant, an attorney, a psychotherapist or a doctor, paying an interpreter for a visit for which you're charging a client $50 or more might appear pretty reasonable.

Some people may not be able to use an interpreter. It's your job to find out by asking them.

Lipreading

Not all people who have lost hearing automatically "lipread," either. Lipreading is a skill; difficult even for those most skilled at it like Jo Waldron, who admits she's unusual in being able to get most of what you're saying through lipreading. Most deaf people who lipread can get only about 30 percent of what's said that way. While some deaf people may be comfortable lipreading when it's a one-on-one situation, as Frank Bowe pointed out, lipreading is an almost impossible way to communicate in a group.

If your deaf client or patron specifies that they do lipread, and says that they prefer that form of communication, ask them what you can do to make their job easier. Don't assume that exaggerating your words with your lips and tongue helps; it may hurt. Obviously, it's important to face the lipreader when you talk. Ask for additional pointers from your deaf patron. Don't be shy about asking for help. It's how you learn. A deaf client will like you better and feel more comfortable with you knowing that you want to do what's right.

Shouting

It isn't just another trick question — but it's not what you should do, either. Many of us think that shouting will help a hard-of-hearing person. In fact, the opposite is true. People with hearing impairments need you to talk in a distinct, well-modulated normal voice. The national group, Self Help for Hard-of-HearingPeople, puts out many pamphlets and videos on working with people who are hard-of-hearing. (See Appendix C.)

Communicating in groups

Often, your contact with deaf patrons isn't a one-on-one situation. You may be presenting a seminar; you don't know in advance if deaf people will be among those attending. You may be putting on a series of lectures. How do you know who will sign up?

The ADA does not require that deaf people who need "auxiliary aids and services" let you know in advance; to do so would be against the purpose of the law that allows people with disabilities the same freedom as any of us to decide at the last minute if they're going to come to a public lecture or any open-to-the-public event. So what do you do?

Assistive listening systems

New places frequently equip their theaters, conference room, presentation area or lecture halls with what the law calls "assistive listening devices." New buildings will be required to install them.

These systems amplify sounds going into microphones and send the audio signals directly to either the hearing aids of listeners, or to small receivers held or worn by the listener. There are several types: An **"FM system"** works just like an FM radio signal, for that's what it is. Costs to equip a conference room with an FM system can range anywhere from $100 or so up to thousands, depending on the size of the room. An **"infrared"** system is similar to the FM system, except that it transmits its audio signals using infrared light, rather than FM signals. Places like the Kennedy Center for the Performing Arts in Washington D.C. and many arts centers use an infrared system. One expert we spoke to said that a "living room size" room could be equipped with the system for around $300.

An **"audio loop"** system relies on a wire to transmit sound from microphones to receivers within the wired area. In new buildings, the wires are put into the walls; for a temporary system, a wire can be run around the perimeter of a room or even around a smaller section of a room. Anyone sitting inside this wired area can pick up the signal being transmitted. These systems can cost from a couple of hundred dollars.

Many hearing aids today are equipped with a telecoil to pick up signals sent through these systems. Listeners with these hearing aids don't need other receivers to pick up the signals. All the systems, however, come with tiny receivers to be worn or placed near a listener who doesn't have a hearing aid but who needs amplification.

If you already have a room equipped with some sort of a public address system, these systems can often be hooked into your present system, saving both labor and costs. When you think about the cost of one of these systems, ask yourself: How much did we pay for our microphones? How much did we pay for our videotape system? The costs are certainly comparable. It's just that we view them differently. Appendix C lists manufacturers of systems .

If you're offering a class or a lecture, deaf attendees must be able to participate the same as the other attendees. What you're required to provide depends on what the deaf attendees need. Because deaf people don't all understand sign language, a qualified interpreter, someone who's registered with the Registry of Interpreters for the Deaf, for example, may not be a complete solution. People who lipread may wish to sit up close to the speakers; you must accommodate such a request. The rule, as we've stated throughout this book, is to check with deaf participants on what they need.

If you are offering a speaking program of any sort that's open to the public and you don't know in advance who may attend, you will need to line up an interpreter for the event. It's best to have an interpreter working at all speaking events, whether any deaf people show up or not. Every state has a registered interpreters; your state association of the deaf will know how to contact them. Or look in the phone book under "interpreters." Fees can range from around $25 an hour on up, depending on what's needed. One interpreter cannot be expected to interpret an entire day's seminar; interpreting is hard work and interpreters need breaks. For longer events, two interpreters (or more) should be hired.

There are other things to learn about working with interpreters, too — things such as where to have an interpreter stand during the lecture; lighting (the interpreter needs to have enough light on him so that deaf members of the audience can see signs clearly.) Sometimes, if technical material is to be presented, an interpreter may need to familiarize himself with it beforehand.

Videotapes and films ; captioning

Films and videotapes can be "open captioned." This means everyone can see the captions. Many of the larger services that prepare and duplicate videotapes can add captions. They may not call them "captions for the deaf," however. Films and videos are captioned for many reasons, including translating them into other languages. When we watch foreign films with subtitles, we're watching open-captioned films. For years, deaf people have enjoyed foreign movies for a reason totally different than those of us who go to the trendy little movie houses that show foreign films! The Caption Center in Boston captions many of today's home videos; they can put open or closed captions on your video or film. (See Appendix C).

The technology to easily caption movie films and videotapes has been invented, says Frank Bowe, but it hasn't been "deployed commercially" yet. The new law should eventually change that. How long it will take, though, is anybody's guess.

Other methods? You can have the tape transcribed and offer a printed copy of the text to deaf people who attend the viewing of the video. For those in your audience who use ASL as their first language, an interpreter standing beside the video, or an interpreter "bubble" edited into the video itself might be a better choice.

What's best? "In a perfect world," says Bowe, every deaf person would have "some portable 'hearing device,' either implanted or carried around, that would give us information regardless of where we are." Not a device to make us hear, but one that translates sounds into signs and words, depending on what works for us. Other gee-whiz! technologies in the works include devices that "tell" a deaf person, electronically, by pulses, what's being said.

You can't wait for every Deaf person to get a personal interpreting device, though. The law says it's your responsibility to make service available to them *now*, just as you do to hearing customers.

Faxes, teletexts and other ways of communicating

Many deaf people, just like hearing businesspersons, are finding fax machines a blessing for transmitting information. Though it's not a substitute for a TDD or for an interpreter for an in-office meeting, people conducting business with deaf people find faxes speed communication, as we all do. Many deaf people now own fax machines; see if your client does. Teletext services will also have to be accessible to deaf and hard-of-hearing people. For more information, contact the ADA Communications Accommodation Project. (Appendix B).

More information on aids for Deaf people

Now that you know some of what's involved, your next job is to contact some of the sources listed in the Appendices, as well as your local association of Deaf people, independent living center or interpreters' group. Talk to them. Now that you know at least some of the ideas they're likely to present, it's your job to ask questions in order to find out what resources are available in your community in terms of interpreters, captioning services, transcription services and so on. The best thing you can do, if you're in the business of presenting lectures, seminars, training events or theater presentations to the public, is to meet with an interpreters' group or association.

Communicating with people who are blind or who have low vision

As Amy Hasbrouck told us earlier, many people who can't see or who have trouble seeing find people irritated at having to read to them material that is provided for other people via visual signs.

"What's the matter, are you blind?" one irritated traveler snapped at Stan Greenberg who stopped him for directions in an airport. "As a matter of fact, I am," Greenberg says he responded.

The law requires you to make your place and your services available to blind people by means of "auxiliary aids" like "qualified" readers and materials on cassette, in large print and braille. We've already discussed some of these methods in other chapters. Part of providing an "accommodation," it should go without saying, is doing it in a pleasant manner that allows the person receiving the service to maintain a sense of dignity. Because a menu, or catalog prices, are being read to a customer is no reason to make that person feel inferior.

Our previous chapter discussed installing signs in braille to accompany all your printed signs — particularly signs in lobbies.

For simple, short transactions in places like stores, health spas and the like, the simplest solution may be to read or tell a blind patron whatever material you hand to sighted patrons, such as a price list or a menu. There are times, however, when the material needs to be kept and referred to by a blind person.

Just as not all deaf people use American Sign Language, not all blind people read braille. In recent years, says Bonnie O'Day, blind children weren't taught braille because of the availability of cassette tapes. Nor do people who become blind in later life often know braille.

Using cassette tapes or readers

For many blind people, material provided on cassette tape offers a solution. Giving a blind person material on cassette allows them independent access to it, and they may peruse it at their own rate. The use of audio cassette-directed tours in art museums is a good example of using casette tapes in public accommodations that works not only for blind people but is in common use for sighted people as well.

There are times, however, when cassette tapes are less practical than providing an on-the-spot reader: when material changes frequently or when the material is short enough to be read in a short length of time. Bonnie O'Day, as director of an independent living center, uses a reader "about six hours a week," she says, having organized the materials she needs read so that things like correspondence, memos, articles and other things a director of an agency needs to read can be handled in one or two weekly sessions. In Boston, says O'Day, the going rate for readers is around $7 an hour.

Do it in large print. It's easy

Many people whose vision is weakening due to age find large-print materials readable.

You can produce large-print documents on your office computer. Simply select "14-point" type size from your word processing or desktop publishing program, and print your menus, price lists or program schedules in that size.

Almost any quick-print shop can enlarge pages of "regular print" to the 14-point type size required for large-print readers, by setting the enlarger to 125% enlargement — unless the original type is very tiny (under 9 point.) Even then, 14-point (or larger) type can be gotten by making an enlargement of your enlargement. Be creative!

As you can see, the cost of making a few large-print copies is barely over 25 cents a page. If you own a copier that enlarges, it's even cheaper. Be sure to let all your patrons know that you provide programs, menus, etc. in larger size print. Put up a sign: "MATERIALS

AVAILABLE IN LARGE PRINT ALSO." You may be surprised how many of your patrons prefer this.

Following the principles of *universal* design, why not choose "large-print" as your standard print size? If the material you print, such as a seminar schedule, a program or a menu or price list, is fairly short, you'll find that the large print requires little more paper.

What about braille?

"People are starting to realize the importance of braille," says Bonnie O'Day. Braille has many advantages over audio recordings, say blind people who use it. Like print, it can be read at the speed of the reader; a reader can turn to specific pages and paragraphs and mark them. Just as it's easier to find things in a printed catalog than on a videotape, so it's easier to find things in braille. "Braille has really been de-emphasized in the past 20 years with mainstreaming" of blind students into public schools along with sighted students, says O'Day. "And what we've seen is a decrease in literacy of blind people." O'Day says that younger blind people, aware of what they've lost out on, are beginning to advocate for the use of braille.

As with anything else, the more widespread a technology is, the less expensive it becomes. Today, personal braille printers are available for under a thousand dollars — though workhorse versions used by commercial braille presses can cost 30 to 40 times that amount. A $250 computer program can translate your word-processed text into braille characters for computer output via a braille printer. (See Appendix C.) With one of those and a personal braille printer (also listed in Appendix C) you can print any of your materials in braille.

But before you set up as a braille printing outfit, we suggest you talk to local groups of blind people. There may already be a local one in operation, saving you time and money. Catalogs, legal information, contracts and the like may be best for your clients and patrons in braille.

A standard page of braille contains about 200 words. The typical size of a braille page is 11 1/2 inches by 11 inches — 3 inches wider than the standard 8 1/2 x 11-inch office paper, says William M. Raeder, head of Boston's National Braille Press, one of the half dozen or so large braille presses in the nation. (See Appendix C). Contact these companies if you need to have catalogs, magazines or complicated materials — or if you need large quantities printed.

For smaller jobs, someone who transcribes into braille may be your best bet. A partial list of people who do this is found in Appendix C. Or you may be able to find someone local who will do the job. Contact your local chapter of the National Federation of the Blind. Your local independent living center may also be able to refer you to someone blind who owns a home or office computer with a braille printer. You may need to deliver your material on computer disk, but with today's computerized homes and businesses, providing a computer disk copy of your seminar agenda, restaurant menu or price list for your shop is probably not too hard for you to do.

Prices for printing materials in braille will depend on the number of copies you want, and how long your piece is. Prices should be comparable to the prices to have someone typeset and print your materials in "ink-print." You may want to shop around and compare prices several individuals offer.

On computer disk

More and more blind people today have computers which read material to them via voice output machines or through their own personal braille printers. Check with a client to see if providing material on computer disk makes it easier for both him and you. Things like tax forms, insurance information, contracts, price lists, catalogs and even copies of correspondence could all be given to a blind client on computer disk if they prefer it that way. Check with your client or patron to see if that option is good for them.

As we have stressed throughout this book: the important thing is to ask your client or patron what will make your service accessible to *them*. To put it another way: you may offer braille catalogs of your products, but if your customer doesn't read braille, you haven't accommodated that client as the law says you must. So it's crucial that you learn what your customer needs.

That doesn't mean you shouldn't be prepared. Making printed materials available in some accessible formats shows you are making a good-faith effort to accommodate people with vision impairments. And, as we've seen in this chapter, that doesn't have to cost a lot.

Communicating with people who can't read or who have trouble understanding

We sometimes forget that not all people can read. People with learning disabilities, people with mental retardation, even people with brain injuries as well as people who have not had the benefit of education need materials in accessible formats, too. While audio and videocassette tapes often make it easier for customers with these difficulties to understand your programs, services and materials, you may also have to spend time one-on-one explaining things in a clear, uncomplicated manner. Acting rushed, uninterested or irritated may hinder your communication.

People who experience psychiatric disabilities may find it difficult to understand the information you're providing if your or your staff's behaviors create an environment for them that seems hostile or threatening. You may wish to get more information on this from one of the groups listed in Appendix B.

Technology will make this chapter obsolete! So read on . . .

Processed information today moves around the world at the literal speed of light, on fiber-optic cables. Satellites catch electronic signals from a speaker in New York and bounce them to Tokyo, where they appear on a TV screen as written text — in Japanese.

The technology already exists to make any information—in any format —available in almost any other format for practically no additional cost. It's not smoke-and-mirrors. It's computerized processing. This book we hold in our hands was, just a few months ago, nothing more than electronic pulses in a computer. It is available to blind people on computer disk — they can put the disk into their computer which has a voice output system and hear what you are reading with your eyes right now. In a few short years, say industry experts, printed books may be on their way to being obsolete. People will own hand held computers like the already-available Sony Discman and read, on user-friendly computer screens, the text of this or any other book. The "books" will be on credit-card size magnetic cards. Blind people will be able to take the cards, install them into computers, and have them display on a moving braille plate of tiny pins—or have their computer read the books in computer-synthesized speech.

Because of the Television Decoder Circuitry Act, passed in 1990, new TVs must contain a "decoder-chip" so that deaf people can see the captions on "closed-captioned" videos — at no extra cost. Many of today's videos and almost all prime-time TV programming — including commercials — are closed-captioned. Expect the technology to do this to become routine — and possibly required — on all videos. Expect it to become something that can be done as easily as pushing a "record" button on your VCR.

Expect more and more services to become available to deaf customers via TDD numbers (Merrill Lynch already offers a TDD stock-quote line) and "videotext services" in coming years. Expect computerized conversions of audiotapes and the audio portion of videotapes into print — and vice versa.

When you read computer and technology reports available to your business, keep on the lookout for this kind of new technology that will, as a byproduct, make the things you offer customers to be "switched" easily from one format (spoken) to another (visual or printed) and vice-versa. Be on the lookout for it, and put yourself in the forefront of your business by learning how this new technology can make your services equally available to everyone you do business with — whether they see or hear or not.

Chapter 7
Remove Barriers & Increase Your Profits!

"Helen" is a 42-year old corporate executive married to a stockbroker. The couple have four children. They live within one mile of a large shopping center that they don't shop at. Why not? "The shopping center isn't accessible. Due to an injury received in a car accident at age 17, Helen is a wheelchair user." June Kailes often tells this story to the groups she trains. It's a typical story, she says.

"The lack of curb cuts, designated parking spaces for people with disabilities and steps into stores force this family to travel 8 miles to shop at a shopping center that they find barrier free," Kailes tells us.

This is only one of many stories disabled people can tell you about how accessible places can bring you increased profits.

"Let's say you owned a store in this inaccessible complex," Kailes continues. "If your average customer sale is $10, and if you average 100 customers a day, then you may be losing $100 in sales daily" from people with mobility problems — based on a conservative estimate that ten percent of your potential customers have mobility impairments, Kailes adds.

Store owners often protest, when asked to install access ramps and lightweight doors, that "we don't have any customers in wheelchairs using our store — why should we spend money on access when no one who needs it shops here?" Look at that remark again. Find something funny there? Of course you don't have any shoppers in wheelchairs if your store isn't accessible! They take one look and go someplace else! You never know they've considered your place.

"The Americans with Disabilities Act is going to benefit everyone," insists Marian Schooling Vessels, head of the Maryland Governor's Committee on Employment of People with Disabilities and a wheelchair user. "When I worked in Annapolis (Annapolis, she adds, is a very old city), there were 10 or 15 restaurants I'd have to pass to go to the one that was ramped. It turned out that the food in that ramped restaurant, though, was wonderful. So I went back again and again. I can tell you that in two or three months' time I gave that restaurant $500 or $600 worth of business — just from me and the people who went with me — because they spent a couple of hundred dollars to make their place accessible." She adds, "We always passed by 15 other possibly-wonderful restaurants which *didn't* get our business. This one restaurant had increased its profits due to me and my friends, because it was accessible."

Many of us with disabilities know what restaurant owners along Washington, D.C.'s Connecticut Avenue may never realize: Many of us, in town for work on the law or other matters, have cruised up and down looking for the one or two of the dozens of restaurants we can dine at, because they have ramped their one or two steps. Those restaurants will often get as many of a dozen of us over a night or two. Word spreads: "So-and-so's place is accessible." Other restaurants never even know they've lost $200 or more *each night* because of their lack of a simple $100 to $1,000 ramp — a cost they could recoup in a week or so, once word gets out that they're accessible. As Kailes puts it: "People don't come in ones. They come in families, in couples, in groups. If your place is inconvenient for one member of that group, chances are nobody in the group is going to shop at your place."

"People with disabilities have economic power," says Vessels. "I don't think business establishments necessarily understand that. People with disabilities have money. We need to purchase services, too. But often we can't, because of physical barriers. I've had businesses say to me, 'no one's ever told me that they wanted to get in.' It's a chicken-and-egg thing. Why haven't I had anyone with a disability in my shop? Well, you haven't because you're not accessible. It's not something that's in the forefront of business owners' minds."

It's often cheaper than you think. All throughout this book, we've offered ideas for relatively low-cost access solutions. We've done that by avoiding special and by accepting do-it-yourself and basic solutions. Still, your reaction may be that things are going to have to cost more than this. "Most of the businesses I've been in touch with in the past six years have had an initial reaction that things are going to cost a lot, and that they have to be 'high-tech' and complicated," says Richard Dodds, who has run United Cerebral Palsy of New Jersey's resource center which has been providing accommodations and "auxiliary aids" for disabled people and businesses for a long time. "But when you start to break down the essence of what's needed," says Dodds, "the majority of things people need aren't high-tech but everyday tech." Dodds tells us the story (which we mentioned in an early chapter) about the man who needed a computer keyboard turned on its side so he could type using his tongue. He needed nothing more high-tech than a wooden frame built to hold a computer keyboard in a vertical position!

Seeing a man with severe cerebral palsy would make most places think that the "accommodation" the man would need would be very expensive — because the man's disability seems so "severe." In fact, the man needed a very inexpensive accommodation. This story is a useful one to keep in mind when you consider costs in general.

Costs are relative

In our previous chapter, we discussed equipping conference areas with infrared listening systems and providing captions on your videotapes. The costs, often in the hundreds of dollars, may have seemed unreasonable to you.

We'd like you to start thinking of these costs in relation to other costs that you incur more readily. How much did your public address system itself cost? Your microphones? Your speakers? Didn't you buy a videotape player, a monitor? Those are all relatively recent costs for businesses. The idea of using videotapes for presentations was unheard of two decades ago. It's a cost no business incurred back then.

But when the technology became available, many of us bought it. Even though it cost our enterprise anywhere from several hundred to thousands of dollars, we got it — because we saw it as a way to increase our services and profits.

We'd like to suggest that at least in some cases, the reluctance we feel in spending money for accommodations has less to do with the actual costs and more to do with what we think it's going to do for business. If it seems like it's something for "them," we feel it's a burden. On the other hand, if it's something we *want*, if it's for us, and our "regular" clients, then it seems like a wise expenditure.

It's time to turn this thinking around. And turning it around is the single best thing you can do for yourself to improve your willingness to serve these new potential groups of patrons.

Tax breaks for making your place accessible

In addition to making good business sense, making expenditures for access need cost you *half—or less*—of the actual price tag because of the credit and deduction available for removing barriers.

Section 44 of the IRS Code: A new Tax Credit

In 1990, concerned that small businesses get as much help as possible in making their places accessible, Congress adopted an important new tax credit for removing barriers in existing buildings, Section 44 of the Internal Revenue Code, the "Disabled Access Credit." As a small business, you're eligible for this credit if you
- have no more than 30 fulltime employees

    or
- have no more than $1 million in gross receipts in a year.

To be eligible for this credit, a small business needs to meet only *one* of the above requirements. You can get a credit of 50 percent of the "eligible access expenditures" (defined below) you make in a tax year, up to a maximum expenditure of $10,250 — but the first $250 you spend is not eligible for the credit. In other words, if you spend just $200 on a ramp, you're not eligible for the tax credit. (You would be eligible for a deduction.) But if you spend $3,250 on a ramp, you are eligible for the tax credit. First, subtract the $250, leaving you with a $3,000 "expenditure." Your tax credit would be 50% of that, or $1,500. The maxiumum credit you can get each year is $5,000.

The IRS defines "eligible access expenditures" as amounts paid or incurred:
- for the purpose of removing architectural, communication, physical or transportation barriers which prevent a business from being accessible to or usable by individuals with disabilities
- to provide qualified interpreters or other effective means of making "aurally delivered" materials available to individuals with hearing impairments
- to provide qualified readers, taped texts, and other effective methods of making visually delivered material avaiable to people with visual impairments
- to acquire or modify equipment or devices for individuals with disabilities
- to provide similar services, modifications, materials or equipment.

In the example above, let's say you spent $1,000 on a ramp and $750 on interpreters in the course of your tax year. Your total expenditures eligible for the Tax Credit would be $1,750 minus the first $250, or $1,500. Fifty percent of that would be $750; you'd get a $750 tax credit. (In effect, the interpreters would end up costing your business nothing!)

To claim this tax credit, use the new IRS form 8826, "Disabled Access Credit." You can obtain the form from your accountant, from your local source for IRS tax forms or by calling the toll-free IRS number, 1-800-829-3676.

Section 190: A tax deduction

You can also, in addition to the Tax Credit, take an annual tax deduction of up to $15,000 each year for removing barriers to disabled individuals "in a place where business or trade is conducted." You can claim this deduction no matter what size your business. This deduction applies to removing barriers at existing places of business. It can include things like grading, sidewalks, parking lots, ramps, entrances, doors, flooring, fixing up restrooms, water fountains, phones, elevators, elevator controls, adding access and braille markings, and so on. Unlike the tax credit, this tax deduction is available for you even if you spend only $100 on access. There is no minimum.

How to use the tax credit and tax deduction to your best advantage

It's best to take the advice of your accountant about how to use these two IRS programs to your best advantage. But an example may help you think about how they can work for you.

Let's say you have spent $12,000 on changing things at your current place to make them accessible. Section 44 allows you to claim a credit of up to $5,000 maximum for your changes. So do that first.

After you've done that, you still have $7,000 worth of expenditures which you can use to claim the tax deduction under Section 190. The amount of the deduction will, of course, depend on your total tax liability. But you can see how an initial outlay of $12,000 can turn into an expenditure of well under $7,000 for your business once you've used both the tax credit and tax deduction.

Chapter 8
Meeting your disability community

"Talk to disabled people. Hear it from them." That's the advice of The Disability Rights Education and Defense Fund's Liz Savage, who has been working with business groups since before the passage of the law to make sure the business community understands and feels comfortable with the changes they're being asked to make. DREDF, the national disability rights legal defense fund which worked intensively on the law and the rules, offers a variety of trainings on the law to both disability and business groups. "We know that businesses don't like the unknown" — and that's understandable, says Savage. "We tell them that the law is flexible *specifically for them.* We know they have concerns," she says. Savage tries to help businesses realize that a lot of their concerns are based on the fact that they've never interacted much with people who have disabilities. "It's not their fault they've never interacted with disabled customers," says Savage. "There have been barriers.

"I try to encourage them not to be inhibited about asking disabled people specific questions. I tell them to always be open, and to understand that this is a training process; that they need to be open to it. I also tell them that a person with a disability is their best source of information."

But not all disabled people may want to be "sources of information." It's important for you to understand why this is — and to understand that there's a right and a wrong way to ask a disabled person for information.

"I get incredibly tired of being the 'educator' —the person who's always supposed to put their personal feelings aside and be ready to explain my life to others," says Deborah McKeen. She looks forward to a day when "I don't have to interact as intimately with strangers as I do now." One of the most frustrating and embarrassing things to McKeen, as it is to many, many people in wheelchairs, is "going up and having to ask, 'do you have an accessible restroom,' and asking it right out in the middle of the restaurant, and having people look at me and not understand what in the world I'm talking about by asking for something called an 'accessible restroom.' "

What usually happens then, says McKeen, is that "people end up asking specific questions about my personal bathroom needs and behavior right there in public. I've had to explain how I go to the bathroom, right there in the restaurant. On a good day I can accept that, and say, 'OK, they don't know any better.' But I'm 42, and I became disabled at age 5. After 37 years of this, it gets old."

McKeen is not alone in resenting what she considers questions in inappropriate settings and personal prying into her life. "People ask questions that are truly none of their business. People are very curious about people with disabilities. Some of it, unfortunately, is prurient interest.

"I remember in junior high school, the school paper said, 'What would happen if Debbie ever stopped smiling?' At the time, I liked it because it made me seem 'nice.' But later I realized what it meant: I have to smile all the time. No one wants to ever see any other part of me than the happy-go-lucky, cheery person who copes so bravely in spite of her disability. That makes me easier for them to deal with. Even now this is still the ultimate example I can think of to explain how nondisabled people regard us. We always have to make it easier for them.

"I've had therapists come up and tell me, 'Debbie, you are so amazing! When I have a bad day, I always think of you and it makes me feel better.' " The remark, meant, no doubt, to be a compliment, is the kind of thing that silently angers many people with disabilties. McKeen speaks for many of us when she says, "I am not courageous. I am not inspiring. I am just going through life, with my own limitations. I truly resent this 'false heroism' stuff. I am not a hero. I have done some great things, and I intend to keep on — but they're not necessarily related to my being disabled. And I resent that I'm viewed only in relation to my disability. I want to be able to interact with people — but I want to do it because I choose to, not because I'm forced to. I really like people. But at times my perceptions of them are marred because I'm so often forced to interact with them from a helper-helpee relationship." That kind of relationship wouldn't have to exist if things were accessible.

"We all have to smile at each other and make inane faces and say inane things." McKeen knows it's usually because people are uncomfortable around people with disabilities and don't know how to interact — but she, like many of us, is tired of always having to be the one who "makes it easy." "They go away thinking they've done their good deed for the day by holding the door open for me, when it would be so much better if I could just get through the door myself. They also get a false picture of who I am as a person." Many disabled people say this. Because they're thrown into situations by our inaccessible society that force them to "ask for favors," they come away looking helpless. "Nondisabled people don't have to do that."

That point — that "nondisabled people don't have to do that" — is a crucial one.

"The nature of the helper-helpee relationship is that there's condescension there," says McKeen. "It can't be helped. You're being condescended to by people who don't even know you — other than having a sense of pity or feeling sorry for you or thinking, 'God, I couldn't live like she does!' They say, 'I'd rather be dead than be like you!' That gets old."

If you think McKeen's analysis is a harsh one, think back to how you'd feel at having to spend 37 years of your life being grateful for getting to go through a door.

Perhaps you, like the people McKeen encounters, want the disabled people you meet to be all smiles and helpfulness. But they, like you, have a right to be crabby. Many of them get tired of explaining their life and needs in detail.

A lot of the frustration people like McKeen feel — and their anger at you for asking personal questions — can be avoided. It has to do with dignity. The best way we can explain it is by looking again at what McKeen calls the "helper-helpee relationship."

If you view a disabled person as someone you're going to help, not an equal, your attitude comes across. If, on the other hand, you view us as equal to your nondisabled customers — and really feel that, that attitude will come across too. Of course, you'll need practice. Disability groups can help you get that practice.

Remember what actress Geri Jewell told us about her experience "educating" the flight attendant? And about how people think she's either courageous, or pitiful; that they mistake her cerebral palsy for evidence that she's mentally retarded — or drunk? "If it were my responsibility to go around changing what other people believe about me," she told us, "I'd still be back in that 7-Eleven convincing someone that I'm not drunk."

Working openly and honestly with members of the disability community can teach us a lot. "Disability creates a discomfort area in all of us," Jewell says. "It's not the disability that we're so uncomfortable with, though. It's guilt and pain. The pain has to do with being human. If we can realize that pain is a part of all of us, we can have the courage to feel it, to walk through it, then we can see people with disabilities" for who they are, as just regular people, she says, "instead of having a perpetual relationship with that pain."

Lorelee Stewart points out that, "The most important thing is to ask the disabled person what they personally need." Every disabled person should be able to tell you that. The key, for you, is to understand that some disabled people are more able to explain access issues than others. And that some like doing that; others don't.

Just like nondisabled people, people who happen to have disabilties do not all think alike. This may seem obvious, but one of the biggest complaints disabled people have is that "they think we're all alike." Whether we have a disability or not, we're all different. I might be liberal, conservative, Democrat, Republican, Catholic, agnostic, highly-educated — or I may have never finished the 6th grade. Some of us are very interested in disability rights and keep up with issues in the disability community; others of us don't even know other disabled people — and may not even consider ourselves "disabled." So, even though we've had a heart attack and really need lightweight doors and in-close parking spots, we may have never even considered the issue. We may still think that those kinds of things are for others to decide for us. "A lot of people don't yet define themselves as 'disabled,' " Stewart adds. "Or, they're newly disabled, and they are not going to know a lot about disability accommodation and access yet."

"The most important thing is to ask the disabled person what they need," says Stewart. "Ask them, 'how can I change things to make it better for you?' They might say something like, 'Actually, if you had a flashing light on that phone I could see it from across the room.' " Their response might surprise you. They may want something that you never thought of. And that's the essence of what is meant by "accommodation" under the Americans with Disabilities Act: It's what works best for *that person.*

Notice, too, that this way of asking is different than the over-eager, voyeuristic questioning about bathroom habits that McKeen so dislikes. As with everything else, there's a right way and a wrong way to ask. Learning this right way and wrong way might be something a disability group could help you with, through role playing. The key is to not seem prying, to treat the disabled person with respect and dignity, to let them be in charge of deciding how much to tell you — and about what.

But although anyone can tell you what they personally want and need, not all of these people would serve your business equally well in giving overall advice about providing access or changing discriminatory practices. "Not every disabled person knows everything that's out there that can benefit them," Stewart reminds us. A lot of people have never gotten out much, have never had a job, "have never even been offered access or accommodations, so it's all a new thing to them, too. There might even be a situation where an employer or store owner would know more about 'access' than a disabled customer."

Some tips

Have a disabled person who knows about access come to your place for a site inspection. Although it's our aim to prepare you as thoroughly as you can to make the changes you need, nothing beats having someone who can actually come to your place, look at your layout and answer specific questions. While it's true that different people will tell you different things, you can generally expect persons with disabilities who work with disability rights groups and who have been active in getting your state's access code passed to be fairly knowledgeable.

It is always preferable to get someone with a disability to talk with you about access and rights issues. But it's equally important that it be someone who has worked with these issues and can explain them.

It is important to avoid non-disabled "consultants" (who may want to charge you a large fee) who have no reputation within the disability community. While someone doesn't have to have a disability to be a good disability consultant, in general your best advice will come from people who have first-hand experience with dealing on a daily basis with the kinds of problems our "experts" in this book have been telling you about.

"My advice to you," says Mike Collins, "is to contact someone you know with a disability, and start there. Get someone from a local disability advocacy group and have them look at your facility." Someone with a disability, says Collins, "will have a greater sensitivity to your local situation and to ideas for access. It's almost impossible for someone [from a national resource group] handling a hotline to see exactly what condition you're in." With a site visit, he stresses, "somebody can show you with the aid of their own mobility limitation, exactly what someone can reach, and so on."

Collins stresses that he recommends "an advocacy group that has knowlege of the Americans with Disabilities Act. There are very few of us working in disability rights who have been able to avoid knowing about this law. It's been a relevant issue in our community. We've worked on developing the rules." Indeed, many of the independent living centers and regional centers listed at the back of this book, as well as many of the people you met in this book, have had a great deal to do with developing the Department of Justice rules which enforce the law. Collins is involved with the Region 10 Disability and Business Technical Assistance Center (Appendix B), based in Olympia, Washington, serving Washington state, Oregon, Idaho and Alaska.

"Independent living centers know how to provide for access. They're the folks who are already doing it best in their own centers," says Lorelee Stewart — because they have to accommodate a large number of people with widely different disabilities, both as members and as staff. And they've had a lot of experience doing it on very meager budgets, she points out. If anyone should know how to provide accommodation inexpensively, it should be a local independent living center.

However, Stewart adds a note of caution it would be well to heed: "Each independent living center has a different flavor; they're not all alike across the country. Not all of them area as good at these things as others are." She adds that many groups of people with specific disabilities, like blindness or deafness, "have chosen to go off on their own," so some independent living centers may not be as able to provide a "cross-disability" perspective as others.

Don't necessarily expect members of the disability community to be able to provide you consistently with contractors or to know specific prices about barrier removal projects, adds Ron Mace. Some independent living centers may know of contractors who have built ramps and done access modification work. But you may find it more useful to rely on the disability groups to give you hands-on understanding of what people with disabilities need in terms of specific barrier removal at your place; then take that information to your usual remodelers—or better yet, have a three-way discussion with you, your contractor and the disabled consultants about access changes. (Don't forget, too, that in order to get the best prices for materials like grab bars and lever handles, avoid "medical" suppliers in favor of regular building supply centers and discount stores.)

Start with the lists in the back of this book. By calling around, you will find a group who can give you a good consultant who has a disability, who comes from the "disability community," who has worked with disability rights issues and who knows how to give you the information you need. Other ways to find groups: look in your Yellow Pages under headings such as "Organizations" or "Disabled" (maybe "Handicapped.") Don't look for groups of a medical nature; look for groups of people with disabilities. A clue: Often "of" is part of the name (like the Anytown Association of the Deaf)—rather than "for." The "of" in the title is your signal that the group is run by people with disabilities; that's usually a better choice. (Though we have stressed using the disability community as sources of information, you need to also check with your national trade group or business association. Many such groups can provide more detailed information on specific areas, such as requirements for hotels or retail shops. Appendix B lists trade associations who are developing materials.)

Ways to use disability consultants

1. To examine your place and give advice (beyond what we have offered here). Talk over with them the plans you've made by using our guide; see what they say. They may have ideas that work better in your situation.

2. To talk with you and your staff about interacting with disabled customers. Beyond the information you've learned in this book, and in this chapter, about how disabled people feel about what they find patronizing or rude behavior, such a session will help break the ice and give you and your staff some experience in working with people with disabilities as equals.

3. To provide role playing: It can be useful to role-play situations, such as verbally offering directions to someone who's blind (a blind consultant can point out when your directions aren't clear); someone in a wheelchair can point out to you subtle ways in which your offers to help may seem too eager and too condescending. Use these opportunities as a way to learn. Nobody expects you to know how to do it. We expect you to be willing to learn, and to listen to those of us with disabilities who can explain it to you. A group such as an independent living center may be willing to set up such a role-playing situation for you.

4. Groups of people with disabilities may have other types of training available. Check with them to see what might benefit you, your staff and your business.

Advertising advantages

There's another way people with disabilities can help: They can spread the word that you're a business that's accessible. They can, in fact, bring you new business. "I had a realtor helping me look for a house," says Steve Weiner. "With the relay service in California, it was easy." The realtor was so impressed with using the relay service, says Weiner, that through the interaction the realtor got more referrals from the center Weiner was running at the time. There's no reason you can't become known to a new group of customers as someone who doesn't discriminate. It can only help your business.

Beware of 'get-rich-quick' consultants

"There are 'consultants' out there who are simply copying off sections of the ADA and selling them to businesses for huge amounts of money, and telling businesses things that are patently untrue," warns Collins. "It isn't fair to business, and it isn't fair to people with disabilities" for these rip-off artists to scare the daylights out of businesses. "It only furthers the animosity that's already there and makes businesses really dislike the law.

"There are law firms out there telling businesses to wait for complaints to pile up before they do anything," Collins continues. "These lawyers are just trying to get business." His alarm is echoed by other people, who tell us that "you can just see the dollar signs in the attorneys' eyes." Most people with disabilities are as disgusted with these shark tactics as you are.

There's a right way and a wrong way to learn how to comply with the law. The Department of Justice, in its rules, makes it clear that asking disabled people what they want is a key element of accommodation.

Before you begin to make changes in earnest, sit down with some people from your local disability community and discuss with them some of the ideas in this book, and let them know what you hope to accomplish. Let them help you. You don't need to lay out huge sums of money for advice. Most disability groups charge only a modest fee for their services. Compare prices. Ask yourself: are you better served by expensive outside consultants with no track record in disability rights? Or by a group who *has a history of working for the rights and access* of disabled people?

Our advice: Be a savvy shopper. Go to the disability community. And use your money for making your place accessible.

Chapter 9
Getting Down to Business:
Planning, Prioritizing
& Avoiding Lawsuits

You now know what you're supposed to do to comply with the Americans with Disabilities Act. You've heard from people with a lot of different disabilities. You've heard from us about attitudes that discriminate. You've gotten ideas about making structural changes, too. And we've given you advice on how to find disabled people to talk to about your place. Now it's time to make a plan and get down to action.

Which barriers do you remove first? The Department of Justice gives this schedule:

First, make your place accessible from the sidewalk, parking lot or bus stop (if one is on your property.).

Second, provide access to the areas in your building where you offer your goods and services to the public.

Third, provide access to restrooms.

Finally, says the Department, "take any other measures to provide access to the goods, services, facilities, privileges, advantages or accommodations of a 'place of public accommodation.' "

Changing things that aren't structural in nature—like instructing your waiters to be agreeable about reading a menu—should be put into effect without further delay.

Now let's look at the priorities listed above in more detail. Some of the ideas below come from the Department of Justice; we've filled out the list to make it clearer and more comprehensive.

Making your place accessible from the sidewalk
1. Provide accessible parking spaces.
2. Put curb cuts in the sidewalks on your own property, from the parking lot or city sidewalks up to your entrance.
3. Widen your entrance, if needed.
4. Make your entrance lighter to open; change its doorknob to a lever

Providing access to the areas in your building where you offer your goods and services to the public.

1. Install ramps between levels in your store or restaurant
2. Adjust the layout of display racks, widen aisles
3. Install brighter lights to help low-vision customers
4. Clearly mark display and product areas to help deaf people find the location of things visually
5. Rearrange tables to allow room for wheelchairs to pass
6. Add braille and raised character signs
7. Widen interior doorways; make doors lighter to open; install levers instead of knobs
8. Add visual alarms

Providing access to your restrooms

1. Make sure there's a wide-enough and unobstructed "path" to the restroom from wherever clients, diners, shoppers are likely to be
2. Move vending machines, furniture that's in the way, trashcans, etc.
3. Widen toilet stalls, and provide easily usable lock in stall for privacy
4. Install grab bars
5. Lower towel, tampax dispensers
6. Install lever handles on faucets
7. Put lever handles on doors
8. Put clear identifying signs aat restroom doors, helping people with mental limitations distinguish "men" from "women"
9. Put an access symbol signs at the restroom doors
10. Put brailled or raised signs at the restroom doors

In Chapters 5 through 7, we looked at how to do each of these. Your task now is to get out a pencil and pad and make a plan.Before you even refer to the above list, though, go back and re-read Chapter 4. It discusses many ways in which your policies and practices may be discriminatory. Make a list of your place's policies and practices that may result in discrimination against people with disabilities. Using Chapter 4, jot down ideas for changing these policies and practices to *nondiscriminatory* ones. When you meet with your disability consultants, discuss these things with them and see what they recommend.

They may see things you've overlooked.

After you've made your list of changes for your policies and practices, you're ready to think about physical changes. Using the above list, go through your place in the same order a customer would — from the parking lot and from the street, noting things you need to change. This will be a *preliminary* list. You'll undoubtedly forget things and leave other things out; that's to be expected. You're new at this.

Next, re-read the chapters which deal with making structural changes like adding ramps and providing "auxiliary aids" like braille menus and interpreters, making special note of the sections which deal with the thing you need to change. For example, "Doors" should make clear exactly what to do about your entrance door and your restroom doors. "Curb cuts and ramps" will give you an idea what's needed both for the curb cut from your parking lot and the ramp you need to install from your bar to your dining area.

After you've re-acquainted yourself with these ideas, it's time to consult with disabled people about your plans. The previous chapter told you how to find and use your disability community. Now turn to the back of this book and find the independent living center nearest you. Call them — or another group or organization made up of people with various kinds of disabilities, such as a state association of disabled people, if you know of one — and see if you can get someone to come out and go through your plans with you.

They will probably see things you've missed. And they may know of local people or sources for the goods you need. Ask for someone who not only can help you figure out access for people in wheelchairs, but someone with knowledge about what it's like for people with other disabilities, for example, people who have low vision or are blind. You also should get advice from people who are deaf or hard-of-hearing. The organization might refer you to another group; or they might have someone on hand to do this. Many independent living centers work closely with people with all sorts of disabilities; a man who uses a cane may work with deaf people daily and so can help you understand what you need and where to get it. National groups and sources listed in the Appendices in the back should be able to offer you assistance, too.

Making a timetable

Once you've gotten an idea of where to find the grab bars you need, the ramp contractor; once you've figured out what brailled items you need and where to get them, it's time to take action. The "public accommodations" section of the law took effect January 26. That means you are *already* supposed to be "accessible to and usable by" disabled people! So don't delay—every day you wait brings an added chance of a disabled person finding you inaccessible, and possibly suing you! Using the priorities listed above, figure out a schedule. This very week, for instance, you can restripe a few parking spots, buy those parking access signs and put them on posts, and arrange to get a ramp built up to your door. That's a start. Within a month you should be able to do many of the things you've noted in your plan — widen the restroom door, for example, remove a toilet stall and add levers to your door handles. You can order a TDD today — after talking to the contacts in Appendix C. In two months, you should be able to achieve most (if not all) of the tasks you've outlined in your plan.

You have two things to juggle—the priorities—and the budget. The sooner you contact members of disability groups and let them know your plans (and ask for their help) the better off you'll be in being able to honestly say, if some disabled person should complain, that you were, indeed, making a good-faith effort to begin complying with the law. Don't put it off — start today!

Announcing your access: add it to your ad!

It's important to tell the public that you're accessible to people with disabilities. The Department of Justice reminds cinemas, for example, to be sure to include the "access symbol" on their ads to let the public know they're accessible to people in wheelchairs (if you are!). Adding the words "accessible to wheelchair users" to your ad leaves no doubt.

- put the access symbol routinely in all your newspaper and TV ads, once you're really accessible (that means your restroom, too)
- add the words, "voice/TDD" routinely to the phone number in your ad (when you've bought your TDD) to let callers know they can reach you via voice or TDD at that number

- give specific access information on your ads, such as "accessible to wheelchair users" or "large print and braille menus available."
- add the above information to your phone messages on a routine basis

Think of these additions to your ads simply as advertising tools to get more customers — because, after all, that's what they are!

Budgeting: "Reasonable accommodation" in action

People with disabilities know, better than anyone, that budgets can be stretched only so far. That's why prioritizing is so important — and why it's important to talk with disabled people.

"We have so little money to run our program that any accommodation would be considered 'unreasonable' under the ADA," says Lorelee Stewart of the Independent Living Center of the North Shore in Lynn, Massachusetts. "But we find a way to do it anyway." (Of the ten people on Stewart's staff, nine have disabilities.)

"Our secretary is hard of hearing. We have a TDD that cost us $169 two years ago. We bought it because we had a lot of deaf people calling in, but this secretary uses it, too." Their secretary, says Stewart, needed "phone flashers " [that flash a light when the phone rings] on all the phones; they cost $3 at Radio Shack. And one accommodation cost us nothing to provide: to enable her to hear things better, we stopped shouting across the room at each other. You walk up to her like a civilized person and speak so she can see and hear you. Before she started working here we used to just yell across the room to each other; it was like a zoo. So that's one accommodation that has cost nothing and has made us all more civilized."

"We have an employee [a quadriplegic who uses a wheelchair and doesn't have much use of his hands] who has a gooseneck phone pole. The phone's receiver is hooked up to this pole. That's what he wanted rather than a headset. The headset would have cost $200 or more through AT&T, but we got this gooseneck thing from an occupational therapist he referred us to; it cost $40. For a desk he has a long conference table, one of those folding ones. We got some of those on-desk filing systems so he doesn't have to open drawers. The table and the files cost us about $60; a new desk would have cost us over

$300." The secretary "has requested an audio loop for staff meetings. That costs $300; so we're saving up to get that." Sometimes, says Stewart, they can't afford everything at once, but they do what they can for each other.

Stewart's independent living center, like most of these centers, can offer good models of how things are made accessible over time, neither bankrupting the organization nor keeping people with disabilities from participating equally. Ask them what they have done.

If you can't do everything at once, ask people with disabilities which things, for your particular kind of public accommodation, are most important. If most of your business with the public is over the phone (though you do have the occasional walk-in client), it may make far more sense to buy a TDD and advertise your TDD number than to install an automatic door opener. On the other hand, if you run a high-traffic record and video store, you may find automating your front door will do a lot to increase goodwill, even though it isn't technically required under the Americans with Disabilities Act — particularly if you tie the new door to some sort of an "accessibility sales promotion" that brings in a slew of new customers.

What's it *really* going to cost?

We have tried to give you an idea of what it's likely to cost you to make various changes in your place by listing in our chapters on barrier removal and "auxiliary aids" typical price figures for similar equipment or changes. These figures are only "ball-park" figures. It's impossible to know every situation. You may find that, with advice from the local disability community, you can find things that are less expensive than those we've listed. Or your situation may require a larger financial outlay. The Americans with Disabilities Act requires you to make only those immediate changes that can be done "without too much difficulty or expense"—and it never requires anything that's so expensive that it becomes what the law calls an "undue burden."

Before you decide a change or an "accommodation" stretches your budget too far, though, re-read our chapter, "Remove Barriers and Increase Your Profits." There are lots of reasons for making your place accessible; the law is only one of them. Increased visibility in the community and increased business are real possibilities, too. We wouldn't say that if we didn't mean it.

When you think you can't make it accessible

What if you simply can't make certain things in your place accessible?

People with disabilities differ in their beliefs about how difficult it really is to make a typical place of public accommodation accessible under the "readily achievable" method required of you right now. So do owners of those places. One owner may see making changes as an opportunity to attract a new clientele; is handy as a do-it-yourselfer and enjoys getting her hands around a hammer, saw and screwdriver now and then. Other owners might find replacing a doorknob daunting and may be overwhelmed by removing and capping a toilet and removing a toilet stall partition. These two owners will have highly different views about what's "readily achievable."

Who decides? A disabled person who can't get into your place, can't get to where your goods or services are provided, or can't use the public restroom you provide may have a different view of what ought to be "readily achievable" in your situation than you did when you decided it wasn't possible for you to remove this or that barrier. In such cases, disabled people might even take you to court.

There are ways to avoid this; ways we have been suggesting all through the book. If you don't think you personally can change something inexpensively, maybe the disabled person who wants access knows how to do it in a way you don't. Take advantage of his — or her — knowledge and skills. Or call a local disability group for help. Chances are they'll help you if you let them know you want to do the right thing. People unfamiliar with the kinds of rough-and-ready access disabled people have learned to work with often assume things will cost far more and be far more complicated than they really are. Ask around. Ask business associates. All of you are going to be facing the same issues. Get together with colleagues and invite disabled people who are good at making access changes to address you as a group and tell you how they put a ramp in, for example, at their own organization or their apartment. Learn from them.

The law requires you to accommodate disabled patrons. If you can't make "readily achievable" changes, it says, you have to use other ways to accommodate them. If you can't make your store accessible, you have to be willing to come out to the curb to handle what they need — take their dry cleaning, for example, or attend to their banking if your bank's not accessible.

Though the law allows this, it's not the ideal. The aim of the law is to allow disabled patrons the *same* services as your other patrons; *integrated* services, with dignity. While these other methods may be allowed as a stop-gap measure, you shouldn't settle for them any more than your disabled patrons want to. If you can't do it all at once, make your place accessible a little at a time. Showing a good-faith effort and letting your patrons know you're working as quickly as you can toward access goes a long way toward gaining for you the goodwill that will prevent the lawsuits that might arise if you appear not to care about whether you serve disabled patrons or not.

How to avoid lawsuits

There are no sure-fire ways to avoid lawsuits under the Americans with Disabilities Act. Even the most accessible, most accommodating service can be sued by a disgruntled customer. But most of the rumors you've heard about disabled people eager to file lawsuits are just that — rumors. Unfortunately, many of these rumors have been circulated by attorneys and other business consultants who want to scare you into hiring them — and paying them lots of money, too — to tell you the things that we've told you in this book, that the disability groups and sources in our Appendices will tell you, free of charge — and which you can get from the Department of Justice's own rules.

Those of us who have worked in the disability rights movement know that most of us with disabilities are not at all eager to file lawsuits or complaints. We want access, not legal hassles. And most of us are only too willing to meet you halfway if it's clear you're showing a good-faith effort.

So how do you show that good-faith effort? By
1. Going through the planning process (above), involving the disability community in your efforts,
     and

2. Working with your employees to ensure that you treat customers, clients or patrons who have disabilities without patronizing them and without offering them separate or different services.

In the early chapters of this book, people with disabilities described the humiliating treatment, segregation and outright hostility they've experienced from people who showed, from their words and actions, that they didn't want to be bothered with anyone with a disability. Learn from these chapters. Ask a disability group for help in changing attitudes at your place. Often these attitudes can be entirely unconscious, the result of years of myths and stereotypes. Though the attitudes are wrong and need to be changed, few of us will fault you if it's clear you are making a sincere effort to change.

The Department of Justice rules that tell you how to obey the law stress consulting with people with disabilities. It is our most important piece of advice, too. Our chapter on that topic should help you learn what you can expect, and what to ask for.

Good-faith efforts and an attitude that treats us as equals will go a long way toward lessening the chances that anyone will want to take you to court. But "effort" and "attitude" alone aren't enough—unless you are, in fact, making some changes. The law is clear about this. Do what you can. If you can't do everything, so be it. But you can't use a smile and friendliness and expect to get out of having to put in a ramp, if you need one and if it's something fairly easy to do. The law does allow you to accommodate us in different ways if making a change like a ramp isn't "readily achievable." But you still have to accommodate us. What this means is that if you really can't afford a ramp, you must still do our drycleaning if we want—but you may have to come outside the store and pick it up from us at the sidewalk. And you'll have to install a doorbell so we can ring and let you know we're there.

Marian Vessels tells the story of a wheelchair user in Washington, D.C. who wanted to get carry-outs from a particular Chinese restaurant—"it was one of the great carry-outs." But, she says, it was a tiny shop; there were no tables in it; it was just a carry-out. And, like many places in Washington, it was in an old building with a flight of steps down from the sidewalk. There was no way that owner could put in a wheelchair lift that wouldn't create an economic hardship on the business. "The owners were very accommodating, though," she says. "They'd bring the order out — but you had to phone ahead to let them know you were there." Working with the customer in the wheelchair, says Vessels, they came up with the idea of installing a doorbell on a post on the sidewalk by the flight of steps, with a sign that read, "for assistance, please ring bell." "And they'd come up and take your order, and then bring it out to you. It was truly a 'reasonable accommodation' — and it worked because both parties were interested in making it work."

If lawsuits do occur, they will occur over this point: you think it's too expensive to put in a ramp, so you say that you'll come to the door; whereas your wheelchair-using customer thinks you can put in a ramp for less than you think, and that your refusing to do it is therefore illegal.

How to avoid this impasse? Make sure it really is too expensive before you decide you can't do it. Get several bids. Check with the disability community. They're often experts on knowing who can do access for cheap — they've had to be. Don't try to get a high bid on a job and, using that bid as an excuse, conclude that providing that ramp isn't "readily achievable." If a disabled person knows a cheaper way to do it, and you refuse, then that *would* be grounds for a lawsuit — one the disabled person would probably win. Nobody needs these kinds of avoidable messes.

Or, putting it another way: don't look for ways to avoid the law. Look for ways to implement it. Believe us: in the end you and your disabled patrons will both be happier.

Appendix A

General Supplemental Information

about the
Americans with Disabilities Act

Title I (Employment)
Materials are available from the Equal Employment Opportunity Commission. To order, call 800-669-3362. This is a recording with various messages about EEOC materials; it takes some time to run through; at its end, however, you may order free the final rules on the employment provisions of the Americans with Disabilities Act.

 Training provided by Mainstream, Inc. 1030 15th St., N.W. Washington, DC 20005 (Voice/TDD): (202) 898-1400

Title III (Public Accommodations)
Final rules on Title III of the Americans with Disabilities Act (including the ADA Accessibility Guidelines) are available from: U.S. Department of Justice
(202) 514-0301 (Voice); (202) 514-0381 (TDD)
or may be downloaded from the Department of Justice computer bulletin board at (202) 514-6193.

ADA Accessibility Guidelines
Architectural and Transportation Barriers Compliance Board Washington, D.C. (800) 872-2253

Technical requirements/new construction
ADA Accessibility Guidelines are available from the Architectural and Transportation Barriers Compliance Board Washington, D.C. (800) 872-2253

Tax forms (for Access Tax Credit; tax deduction)
Internal Revenue Service
tax forms ordering service (800) 829-3676

Appendix B
Sources for advice, consultation and information

ADA Regional
Disability & Business Technical Assistance Centers

Region 1
Connecticut, Maine, Massachusetts, New Hampshire, Rhode Island and Vermont
ADA Technical Assistance Center
University of Southern Maine
Muskie Inst. of Public Affairs
Portland ME (207) 780-4430

Region 2
New York, New Jersey, Puerto Rico
ADA Technical Assistance Center
United Cerebral Palsy Assn. of NJ
Trenton NJ (609) 392-4004

Region 3
Delaware, Washington, D.C., Maryland, Pennsylvania, Virginia, West Virginia
ADA Technical Assistance Center
Endependence Ctr of Northern Va.
Arlington VA (703) 525-3268

Region 4
Alabama, Florida, Georgia, Kentucky, Mississippi, North Carolina, South Carolina, Tennessee
ADA Technical Assistance Center
UCP SMART Exchange Atlanta
GA (800) 762-7843

Region 5
Illinois, Indiana, Michigan, Minnesota, Ohio, Wisconsin
ADA Technical Assistance Center
Univ. of Chicago DD Program
Chicago IL (800) 729-8275

Region 6
Arkansas, Louisiana, New Mexico, Oklahoma, Texas
ADA Technical Assistance Center
Independent Living Res.Utilization
Houston TX (713) 520-0232

Region 7
Iowa, Kansas, Nebraska, Missouri
ADA Technical Assistance Center
University of Missouri/Columbia
Columbia MO (314) 882-3807

Region 8
Colorado, Montana, North Dakota, South Dakota, Utah, Wyoming
ADA Technical Assistance Center
Meeting the Challenge, Inc.
Colorado Spgs CO (800) 735-4232

Region 9
Arizona, California, Hawaii, Nevada
ADA Technical Assistance Center
Berkeley Planning Associates
Oakland CA (415) 465-7884

Region 10
Alaska, Idaho, Oregon, Washington
ADA Technical Assistance Center
Washington Governor's Cmte.
Olympia WA (800) 435-7232

National disability groups

Disability Rights Education & Defense Fund Washington DC (800) 466-4232

National Federation of the Blind Baltimore MD (301) 659-9314

Communications Accommodation Project Wash. DC (202) 651-5343

American Foundation for the Blind Washington DC (202) 223-0101

Paralyzed Veterans of America Washington DC (202) 872-1300

Business and trade associations

U. S. Chamber of Commerce Washington DC (800) 638-6582

Council of Better Business Bureaus Arlington VA (703) 276-0100

Building Owners and Managers Association, International
(Government and Industry Affairs) Washington DC (202) 408-2684

National Restaurant Association Washington DC (202) 331-5985

Food Marketing Institute Washington DC (202) 429-4523

American Hotel and Motel Association Washington DC (202) 289-3100

Local disability organizations, by state
(partial list)

Alabama

Independent Living Center 3421 Fifth Ave. South Birmingham AL 35222
(Voice): (205) 251-2223 (TDD): 251-0605

Alaska

Access Alaska 3710 Woodland Drive Anchorage AK 99517 (Voice):
(907) 248-4777 (TDD): 248-0638

Southeast Alaska Independent Living 9085 Glacier Hwy Juneau AK
99801 (Voice): (907) 789-9665 (TDD): 789-9597

Arizona

Arizona Bridge to Independent Living 1229 East Washington Street
Phoenix AZ 85034 (Voice): (602) 256-2245 (TDD): 256-2245

Community Outreach Program for the Deaf 268 W. Adams Street Tucson
AZ 85705 (Voice): (602) 792-1906 (TDD): 792-1906

Disability Resource Center 1023 N. Tyndall Ave. Tucson AZ 85719
(Voice): (602) 624-6452 (TDD): 624-6452

Services to Advance Independent Living 1700 South First Avenue Yuma
AZ 85364 (Voice): (602) 783-3308 (TDD): 783-3308

Arkansas

Mainstream Living 1501 South Main Little Rock AR 72202 (Voice/
TDD): (501) 371-0012

California

Dayle McIntosh Center 150 W. Cerritos Bldg. 4 Anaheim CA 92805
(Voice): (714) 772-8285 (TDD): 772-8366

Darrell McDaniel Independent Living Center 18 South Chester
Bakersfield CA 93304 (Voice): (805) 325-1063 (TDD): 325-3092

Center for Independent Living 2539 Telegraph Ave. Berkeley CA 94704
(Voice): (415) 841-4776 (TDD): 848-3101

Independent Living Services of Northern CA 555 Rio Lindo Ave. Suite B
Chico CA 95926 (Voice): (916) 893-8527 (TDD): 893-8527

Center for Independent Living 408 S. Grand Ave. Covina CA 91723
(Voice): (818) 339-1278 (TDD): 966-8115

Humboldt Access Project 2107 3rd Street Eureka CA 95501
(Voice): (707) 445-8404 (TDD): 445-8404

California Assoc. of the Physically Handicapped 1617 E. Saginaw Way
Fresno CA 93704 (Voice): (209) 222-2274 (TDD): 222-2396

F.R.E.E.D. 154 Hughes Rd. #1 Grass Valley CA 95945 (Voice): (916)
272-1732 (TDD): 272-1733

Community Resources for Independent Living 439 A Street Hayward CA
94541 (Voice): (415) 881-5743 (TDD): 881-5743

Westside Center for Independent Living 12901 Venice Blvd. Los Angeles
CA 90066 (Voice): (213) 390-3611 (TDD): 398-9204

Resources for Independent Living 1211 H Street #B Sacramento CA
95814 (Voice): (916) 446-3074 (TDD): 446-3074

Community Resources for the Disabled 234 Capitol St. Salinas CA 95060
408 757-2968 (TDD): 757-2968

Rolling Start 443 W. 4th St. San Bernadino CA 92401 (Voice): (714)
884-2129 (TDD): 884-0937

Community Service Center for the Disabled 1295 University Ave. San
Diego CA 92103-3333 (Voice): (619) 293-3500 (TDD): 293-7757

Independent Living Resource Center of San Francisco 70 Tenth Street
San Francisco CA 94103 (Voice): (415) 863-0581 (TDD): 863-1367

Independent Living Resource Center 423 W. Victoria Santa Barbara CA
93101 (Voice): (805) 963-1359 (TDD): 963-0595

Adult Independence Development Center 1190 Benton St. Santa Clara
CA 95050 (Voice): (408) 985-1243 (TDD): 985-9243

Community Resources for the Disabled 340 Soquel Ave. Suite 115 Santa
Cruz CA 95060 (Voice): (408) 429-9969 (TDD): 688-0364

Community Resources for Independence 2999 Cleveland Ave. Santa
Rosa CA 95403-2715 (Voice): (707) 528-2745 (TDD): 528-2151

Independent Living Center of Southern California 14402 Haynes Street
Van Nuys CA 91401 (Voice): (818) 988-9525 (TDD): 988-3533

Colorado

Center for People with Disabilities 948 North Street Boulder CO 80302
(Voice): (303) 442-8662 (TDD): 442-8662

Atlantis Community 1120 North Circle Drive Colorado Springs CO
80909-3101 (Voice): (719) 520-9511 (TDD): 520-9514

Atlantis Community 12 Broadway Denver CO 80203-3195
(Voice): (303) 733-9324

Counseling/Hearing Impaired People 4353 Colfax Ave. Denver CO
80220 (Voice): (303) 320-5701 (TDD: 320-5701

Denver Center for Independent Living 455 Sherman Street Suite 140
Denver CO 80203 (Voice): (303) 698-1900 (TDD): 698-1900

The Center on Deafness 11 South Jersey Denver CO 80224
(Voice): (303) 839-8022 (TDD): 839-8022

Center for Independence 835 Colorado Ave. Grand Junction CO 81501
   (Voice): (303) 241-0315 (TDD): 241-0315

Choices for Independent Living 1020 9th St. Suite 206 Greeley CO
   80631 (Voice): (303) 356-3326 (TDD): 356-3326

Northern Colorado Center on Deafness 800 Eighth Ave. Suite 141
   Greeley CO 80631 (Voice): (303) 352-8682 (TDD): 352-8682

Connecticut

Independence Unlimited 900 Asylum Ave. #490 Hartford CT 06105
   (Voice): (203) 549-1330 (TDD): 549-3915

Center for Independence & Access 105 Court Street New Haven CT
   06515 (Voice): (203) 562-3924 (TDD): 562-3924

New Horizons 37 Bliss Memorial Road Unionville CT 06085 (Voice):
   (203) 675-4711

Independence Northwest 581 Wolcott Street Waterbury CT 06705
   (Voice): (203) 573-1080 (TDD): 573-1080

Delaware

Independent Living 818 South Broom Street Wilmington DE 19805
   (Voice): (302) 429-6693

District of Columbia

D.C. Center for Independent Living 1400 Florida Ave. N.E. #3
   Washington DC 20002 (Voice): (202) 388-0033 (TDD): 388-0033

Florida

Pinellas Center for the Visually Impaired 1610 N. Myrtle Ave. Clearwater
   FL 34615 (Voice): (813) 461-4006

Briarwood Center for Independent Living 1023 S.E. Fourth Avenue
   GainesvIndependent Livingle FL 32601 (Voice): (904) 378-7474
   (TDD): 378-7444

Center for Survival & Independent Living (C-SAIL) 1335 N.W. 14th St.
   Miami FL 33125 (Voice): (305) 547-5444 (TDD): 547-5446

Center for Independent Living of Northwest Florida 513 E. Fairfield Dr. Pensacola FL 32503 (Voice): (904) 435-9343 (TDD): 435-9328

Space Coast Association of the Physically Handicapped 1825A Cogswell Rockledge FL 32955 (Voice): (407) 633-6182 (TDD): 633-6282

Center for Independent Living of Northern Florida 1380 Ocala Road Tallahassee FL 32303 (Voice): (904) 575-9621 (TDD): 575-9621

Self-Reliance Center for Independent Living 12310 North Nebraska Ave. Tampa FL 33612 (Voice): (813) 977-6338 (TDD): 977-6368

Center for Independent Living in Central Fla. 720 North Denning Dr. Winter Park FL 32789 (Voice): (407) 623-1070 (TDD): 623-1185

Georgia

Independent Living Program P.O. Box 1606 Albany GA 31702 (Voice): (912) 430-4947

Atlanta Center for Independent Living 1201 Glenwood Ave. SE Atlanta GA 30316 (Voice): (404) 656-2952 (TDD): 656-5911

Heart of Georgia Independent Living Program 707 Pine Street Macon GA 31208 (Voice): (912) 751-6270

Independent Living Program PO Box 13427 Savannah GA 31416-0427 (Voice): (912) 356-2124

Hawaii

Big Island Center for Independent Living 1190 Waianuenue Ave. Hilo HI 96720-2020 (Voice): (808) 935-3777 (TDD): 935-37777

Hawaii Center for Independent Living 677 Ala Moana Blvd #118 Honolulu HI 96813-5407 (Voice): (808) 537-1941 (TDD): 521-4400

Kona Center for Independent Living 75-159 Lunapule Rd. Unit #5 Kailua-Kona HI 96740 (Voice): (808) 329-6611 (TDD): 329-6611

Kauai Center for Independent Living PO Box 3529 Lihue HI 96766 (Voice): (808) 245-4034 (TDD): 245-4164

Maui Center for Independent Living 1446-D Lower Main St. Room 105 Wailuku HI 96793 (Voice): (808) 242-4966 (TDD): 242-4968

Idaho

Dawn Enterprises PO Box 388 Blackfoot ID 83221
(Voice): (208) 785-5890

Living Independence Network Corp. 708 West Franklin St. Boise ID
83702 (Voice): (208) 336-3335

North Idaho Center for Independent Living 124 East Third Street
Moscow ID 83843 (Voice): (208) 883-0523 (TDD): 883-0523

Center Resources for Independent People PO Box 4185 Pocatello ID
83201 (Voice): (208) 232-2747 (TDD): 232-2747

Living Independence Network Corp. 1002 Shoshone Street East
Twin Falls ID 83301 (Voice): (208) 733-1712 (TDD): 733-1712

Illinois

Impact Center for Independent Living 2735 East Broadway Alton IL
62002-1859 (Voice): (618) 462-1411 (TDD): 462-1411

LINC 10 East Washington Belleville IL 62226 (Voice): (618) 235-9988

Living Independence 1328 E. Empire Bloomington IL 61701 (Voice):
(309) 663-5433

Southern Illinois Center for Independent Living 780 East Grand Avenue
Carbondale IL 62901 (Voice): (618) 457-3318 (TDD): 457-3316

Access Living of Metro Chicago 310 South Peoria Suite 201 Chicago IL
60607 (Voice): (312) 226-5900 (TDD): 226-1687

OPTIONS Center for Independent Living 53 Meadowview Center
Kankakee IL 60901 (Voice): (815) 936-0100 (TDD): 936-0132

Opportunities for Access 3300 Broadway Suite 5 Mt. Vernon IL 62864
618 244-9212 (TDD): 224-9575

Central Illinois Center f/Indepen. 4806 North Sheridan Road Peoria IL
61614 (Voice): (309) 682-3500 (TDD): 682-3567

RAMP 1040 North 2nd. Street Lower level Rockford IL 61107 (Voice):
(815) 968-7467 (TDD): 968-7467

Springfield Center for Independent Living 426 West Jefferson Springfield IL 62702 (Voice): (217) 523-2587 (TDD): 523-2587

P.A.C.E. 1717 Philo Rd. Suite 27 Urbana IL 61801 (Voice): (217) 344-5433 (TDD): 344-5024

Indiana

Center for Independent Living 5800 Fairfield Suite 210 Fort Wayne IN 46807 (Voice): (219) 745-5491

Indianapolis Resource Center for Independent Living 2511 E. 46th St. #V4 Indianapolis IN 46205-2452 (Voice): (317) 541-0611

Iowa

Center for Independent Living 524 4th Street Des Moines IA 50309 (Voice): (515) 281-7999 (TDD): 281-7999

Independent Living 26 East Market Iowa City IA 52240 (Voice): (319) 338-3870 (TDD): 338-3870

Kansas

LINK PO Box 1016 Hays KS 67601 (Voice/TDD): (913) 625-6942

Independence 1910 Haskell Lawrence KS 66046 (Voice): (913) 841-0333 (TDD): 841-1046

Resource Center for Independent Living 122 South Sixth Osage City KS 66523 (Voice): (913) 528-3105 (TDD): 528-3106

Independent Connection 1710 W. Schilling Road Salina KS 67401 (Voice): (913) 827-9383 (TDD): 827-9383

Topeka Independent Living Resource Center 3258 South Topeka Topeka KS 66611-2240 (Voice): (913) 267-7100 (TDD): 267-7100

Three Rivers Independent Living Resource Center 810 4th St. Wamego KS 66547 (Voice): (913) 456-9915 (TDD): 456-9915

Independent Living Center of Southcentral Kansas 4808 West 9th Wichita KS 67212 (Voice): (316) 942-8079 (TDD): 942-9027

Kentucky

Contact Inc. 212 W. Broadway Frankfort KY 40601 (Voice): (502) 875-5777

Center for Accessible Living 981 South Third Street Suite 102 Louisville
KY 40203 (Voice): (502) 589-6620 (TDD): 589-3980

Center for Independent Living 1900 Brownsboro Road Louisville KY
40206 (Voice): (502) 893-0211 (TDD): none

Center for Independent Living (Murray Office) 104 North Fifth Street
Suite 203 Murray KY 42071 (Voice): (502) 759-9227

Louisiana

Southwest Louisiana Independence Center 3104 Enterprise Blvd
Lake Charles LA 70601 (Voice): (318) 474-1111 (TDD): 439-294

Independent Living Center 320 North Carrollton Ave. Suite 2C New
Orleans LA 70119 (Voice): (504) 484-6400 (TDD): 484-6400

New Horizons 4030 Wallace Ave. Shreveport LA 71108
(Voice): (318) 635-3652 (TDD): 635-3488

Maine

Maine Independent Living Services 74 Winthrop St. Augusta ME 04330
(Voice): (207) 622-5434 (TDD): 622-5434

Alpha One 85 E Street Suite 1 S. Portland ME 04106
(Voice): (207) 767-2189 (TDD): 767-2189

Maryland

Maryland Center for Independent Living 6305-A Sherwood Road
Baltimore MD 21239-1540 (Voice): (301) 377-5900 (TDD): 377-4591

Massachusetts

D.E.A.F. Inc. 215 Brighton Ave. Allston MA 02134
(Voice): (617) 254-4041 (TDD): 254-4041

Stavros Inc. 691 South East Street Amherst MA 01002
(Voice): (413) 256-0473 (TDD): 256-0473

Boston Center for Independent Living 95 Berkeley St. Suite 206
Boston MA 02116 (Voice): (617) 338-6665 (TDD): 338-6662

Independence Associates 55 City Hall Plaza Brockton MA 02401
(Voice): (617) 559-9091 (TDD): 559-9091

Southeast Center for Independent Living 170 Pleasant St. 3rd Floor East
Fall River MA 02721 (Voice): (508) 679-9210 (TDD): 679-9210

Cape Organization for the Rights of the Disabled PO Box 954
Hyannis MA 02601 (Voice/TDD): (508) 775-8300

The Northeast Independent Living Program 130 Parker Street Lower
Level Lawrence MA 01843 (Voice): (617) 687-4288 (TDD): 687-4288

Renaissance Program 21 Branch Street Lowell MA 01851
(Voice): (508) 454-7944

Independent Living Center of the North Shore 583 Chestnut Street Suite 9
Lynn MA 01904 (Voice): (617) 593-7500 (TDD): 593-7500

AD LIB 442 North St. Pittsfield MA 01201 (Voice): (413) 442-7047
(TDD): 442-7158

Center for Living and Working 484 Main St. #345 Worcester MA 01608
(Voice): (508) 798-0350 (TDD): 798-0350

Michigan

Ann Arbor Center for Independent Living 2568 Packard; Georgetown
Mall Ann Arbor MI 48104 (Voice): (313) 971-0277 (TDD): 971-0310

Southeastern Michigan Center for Independent Living 1200 6th Ave.
11th Floor S. Tower Detroit MI 48226 (Voice): (313) 256-1524

Upper Peninsula Commity for Independent Living 1919 1/2 Fourteenth
Ave. N. Escanaba MI 49829 (Voice): (906)789-0155 (TDD): 789-0156

Grand Rapids Center for Independent Living 3375 S. Division Grand
Rapids MI 49508 (Voice): (616) 243-0846 (TDD): 243-0846

Kalamazoo Center for Independent Living 4026 South Westnedge
Kalamazoo MI 49008 (Voice): (616) 345-1516 (TDD): 345-8022

Center of Handicapper Affairs 918 Southland Street Lansing MI 48910
(Voice): (517) 393-0305 (TDD): 393-0326

Cristo Rey Hispanic Center for Independent Living 1717 North High St.
Lansing MI 48906 (Voice): (517) 372-4700 (TDD): 372-4700

Midland Independent Living Program 1015 Ashman Midland MI 48640 (Voice): (517) 835-4041 (TDD): 835-4041

Blue Water Center for Independent Living 804 Huron Ave. Port Huron MI 48060 (Voice): (313) 987-9337 (TDD): 987-9337

Oakland/Macomb Center for Independent Living 6044 Rochester Road Troy MI 48098 (Voice): (313) 828-3500 (TDD): 828-3310

Minnesota

Center for Independent Living of Northeast Minnesota 205 West Second Street #442 Duluth MN 55802 (Voice/TDD): (218) 722-8911

OPTIONS Interstate Resource Center for Independent Living 211 DeMers Ave. E. Grand Forks MN 56721 (Voice/TDD): (218) 773-6100

Southern Minnesota Independent Living Enterprises & Services 709 S. Front Street Mankato MN 56001 (Voice/TDD): (507) 345-7139

Southwestern Center for Independent Living 317 West Main St. Marshall MN 56258 (Voice): (507) 532-2221 (TDD): 532-2222

Independence Crossroads 1073 Tenth Ave. SE Minneapolis MN 55414 (Voice): (612) 378-0027 (TDD): 378-0027

Freedom Resource Center for Independent Living 725 Center Avenue Moorhead MN 56560 (Voice): (281) 236-0459

Southeastern Minnesota Center for Independent Living 1306 7th St. N.W. Rochester MN 55901 (Voice): (507) 285-1815 (TDD): 285-1815

People Too—Central Minnesota Center for Independent Living 600 25th Ave. S. Suite 110 St. Cloud MN 56301 (Voice/TDD): (612) 255-1882

Accessible Space 2550 University Ave. West #301N St. Paul MN 55114 (Voice): (612) 645-7271 (TDD): none

Metropolitan Center for Independent Living 1619 Dayton Avenue St. Paul MN 55104 (Voice): (612) 646-8342 (TDD): 646-8342

Minnesota State Services for the Blind 1745 University Ave. St. Paul MN 55104 (Voice): (612) 297-2467

Mississippi

Jackson Independent Living Center 300 Capers Avenue Jackson MS
39203 (Voice): (601) 961-4140 (TDD): 961-4140

Missouri

Services for Independent Living 1301 Vandiver Dr. Suite Q
Columbia MO 65202 (Voice): (314) 874-1646 (TDD): 874-1646

The WHOLE PERSON 6301 Rockhill Rd. Suite 305E Kansas City MO
64131 (Voice): (816) 361-0304 (TDD): 361-7749

Southwest Center for Independent Living 1856 East Cinderella Suite E
Springfield MO 65804 (Voice): (417) 886-1188 (TDD): 886-1188

Paraquad 4475 Castleman St. Louis MO 63110 (Voice): (314) 776-4475
(TDD): 776-4415

Disabled Citizens Alliance for Independence Box 675 Viburnum MO
65566 (Voice): (314) 244-3315 (TDD): 244-3315

Montana

Yellowstone Valley Center for Independent Living 3304 Second Avenue
North Billings MT 59101 (Voice): (406) 259-5181 (TDD): 259-5181

North Central Independent Living Services 104 Second St. South
Suite 201 Great Falls MT 59405 (Voice/TDD): (406) 452-9834

Montana Independent Living Project 38 South Last Chance Gulch
Helena MT 59601 (Voice): (406) 442-5755 (TDD): 442-5756

Summit Independent Living Center 1280 South Third Street West
Missoula MT 59801 (Voice): (406) 728-1630 (TDD): 728-1630

Nebraska

Goodwill Center for Independent Living 1804 S. Edd Grand Island NE
68801 (Voice): (308) 384-7896 (TDD): 384-7896

League of Human Dignity 1701 P Street Lincoln NE 68508-1741
(Voice): (402) 471-7871 (TDD): 471-7871

League of Human Dignity Independent Living Center 5017 Leavenworth
Omaha NE 68106 (Voice): (402) 558-3411

Nevada

Nevada Association for the Handicapped 6200 W. Oakey Las Vegas NV
   89102 (Voice): (702) 870-7050 (TDD): 870-7050

Northern Nevada Center for Independent Living 624 East 4th Street
   Reno NV 89512-3401 (Voice): (702) 328-8000 (TDD): 328-8006

New Hampshire

Granite State Independent Living Foundation 172 Pembroke Road
   Concord NH 03301 (Voice): (603) 228-9680 (TDD): 228-9680

New Jersey

Success Through Independent Living Experience 1501 Park Avenue
   Asbury Park NJ 07712 Voice: (201) 774-4737

D.I.A.L. for Independent Living 66 Mt Prospect Ave.- Bldg. C
   Clifton NJ 07013-1918 (Voice): (201) 470-8090

HIP 44 Armory Street Englewood NJ 07631 (Voice): (201) 568-0906

Monmouth/Ocean Independent Living Center 279 Broadway
   Long Branch NJ 07740 (Voice): (201) 571-4884 (TDD): 571-4878

D.I.A.L. (Newark/Union) 32 Park Place Newark NJ 07102
   (Voice): (201) 824-4009 (TDD): 824-3614

NJ Commission for the Blind—Independent Living Service
   1100 Raymond Blvd. Newark NJ 07102 (Voice): (201) 648-3333

Center for Independent Living of South Jersey 800 N. Delsea Drive
   Westville NJ 08093 (Voice): (609) 853-6490 (TDD): 853-7602

New Mexico

C.A.S.A. Box 36910 Albuquerque NM 87176 (Voice): (505) 298-7609

Independent Living Resource Center 2520 Virginia NE Suite 200
   Albuquerque NM 87110 (Voice): (505) 271-1565 (TDD): 271-1565

Disability Resource Center 205 West Boutz Bldg. 4 Las Cruces NM
   88005 (Voice): (505) 526-5016 (TDD): 526-5016

New Vistas—Independent Living Center Ark Plaza 2025 S Pacheco
Santa Fe NM 87501 (Voice): (505) 471-1001 (TDD): 471-3131

New York

Capital District Center for Independence 845 Central Ave. Albany NY
12206-1504 (Voice): (518) 459-6422 (TDD): 459-6422

Independent Living Center of Amsterdam 135 Guy Park Ave.
Amsterdam NY 12010 (Voice): (518) 842-3561 (TDD): 842-3593

Options for Independence 55 Market Street Auburn NY 13021
(Voice): (315) 255-3447 (TDD): 255-2156

Batavia Center for Independent Living 61 Swan Street Batavia NY 14020
(Voice): (716) 343-4524 (TDD): 343-4524

Southern Tier Independence Center 107 Chenango St. Binghamton NY
13901 (Voice): (607) 724-2111 (TDD): 724-2111

Bronx Independent Living Services 3525 Decatur Avenue Bronx NY
10467 (Voice): (212) 515-2800 (TDD): 515-2803

Brooklyn Center for Independence 408 Jay St. Brooklyn NY 11201
(Voice): (718) 625-7500 (TDD): 625-7712

Buffalo Independent Living Center 3108 Main St. Buffalo NY 14214
(Voice): (716) 836-0822 (TDD): 836-0822

Access to Independence and Mobility 271 E First St. Corning NY 14830
(Voice): (607) 962-8225 (TDD): 962-4235

Western New York Independent Living Program 2015 Transit Elma NY
14059 (Voice): (716) 838-6904

Finger Lakes Independence Center 609 W. Clinton Street Suite 112
Ithaca NY 14850 (Voice): (607) 272-2433 (TDD): 272-2433

Queens Independent Living Center 140-40 Queens Blvd. Jamaica NY
11437 (Voice): (718) 658-2526 (TDD): 658-4720

Southwestern Independent Living Center 878 N Main Street
Jamestown NY 14701 (Voice): (716) 661-3010 (TDD): 661-3012

Resource Center for Accessible Living 602 Albany Avenue Kingston NY
12401 (Voice): (914) 331-0541 (TDD): 331-8680

Long Island Center for Independent Living 3601 Hempstead Turnpike Levittown NY 11756 (Voice): (516) 796-0144 (TDD): 796-0135

Massena Independent Living Center 1 North Main Street Massena NY 13662 (Voice): (315) 764-9442 (TDD): 764-9442

Self Initiated Living Options 3241 Route 112 Medford NY 11763-1411 (Voice): (516) 698-1310 (TDD): 698-1392

Barrier Free Living 270 East Second Street New York NY 10009 (Voice): (212) 677-6668 (TDD): 677-6668

Center for Independence of the Disabled in New York 841 Broadway New York NY 10003 (Voice): (212) 674-2300 (TDD): 674-2300

Niagara Frontier Center for Independent Living 1522 Main Street Niagara Falls NY 14305 (Voice): (710) 284-2452 (TDD): 284-2452

Directions in Independent Living 2636 W. State St. Suites A & B Olean NY 14760 (Voice): (716) 373-4602 (TDD): 373-4602

North Country Center for Independent Living 159 Margaret St. STE 202 Plattsburgh NY 12901 (Voice): (518) 563-9058 (TDD): 563-9058

Taconic Resources for Independence 82 Washington St. #107 Poughkeepsie NY 12601 (Voice): (914) 452-3913 (TDD): 485-8110

Rochester Center for Independent Living 758 South Avenue Rochester NY 14620-2237 (Voice): (716) 442-6470 (TDD): 442-6470

Independent Living in the Capital District 2660 Albany St. Schenectady NY 12304 (Voice): (518) 393-2412

Western Orange Co. Center for Independent Living Route 6 Slate Hill NY 10973 (Voice): (914) 355-2030 (TDD): 355-2060

Rockland Independent Living Center 235 North Main Street Suite 13 Spring Valley NY 10977 (Voice): (914) 426-0707 (TDD): 426-1180

Staten Island Center for Independent Living 150 Walker Street Staten Island NY 10302 (Voice): (718) 720-9016 (TDD): 667-1216

ARISE 501 E. Fayette St. Syracuse NY 13202 (Voice): (315) 472-3171 (TDD): 472-3171

Troy Resource Center for Independent Living Broadway & 4th Street Troy NY 12180 (Voice): (518) 274-0701 (TDD): 274-0701

Resource Center for Independent Living 401 Columbia St. Utica NY
13502 (Voice): (315) 797-4642 (TDD): 797-4642

Northern Regional Center for Independent Living Suite 400 Woolworth
Building Watertown NY 13601 (Voice/TDD): (315) 785-8703

Westchester County Independent Living Center 297 Knollwood Road
White Plains NY 10607 (Voice): (914) 682-3926 (TDD): 682-0926

North Carolina

Programs for Accessible Living 1012 S Kings Dr. G-2 Charlotte NC
28283 (Voice): (704) 375-3977 (TDD): 375-3977

Live Independently Networking Ctr. PO Box 389 Newton NC 28658
(Voice): (704) 465-8484 (TDD): 465-8369

North Dakota

Center for Independent Living 1007 N.W. 18th Mandan ND 58554
(Voice): (701) 663-0376 (TDD): 663-0376

Ohio

Tri-County Independent Living Center 414 Pine St. #5 Akron OH 44307
(Voice): (216) 762-0007

Independent Living Options 2433 Harrison Ave. Cincinnati OH 45211
(Voice): (513) 661-2600

Services for Independent Living 25100 Euclid Ave. Suite 105
Cleveland OH 44117 (Voice): (216) 731-1529 (TDD): 731-1529

Mid-Ohio Board Independent Living 1393 E. Broad St. Columbus OH
43205 (Voice): (614) 252-1661 (TDD): 252-1665

Ability Center of Greater Toledo 5605 Monroe Sylvania OH 43560
(Voice): (419) 885-5733 (TDD): 885-5733

Oklahoma

Caddo County Independent Living Program 132 East Broadway Street
#208 Anadarko OK 73005 (Voice): (405) 247-7331 (TDD): 247-7331

Green Country Independent Living Resource Center 310 S. Osage
  Bartlesville OK 74005 (Voice/TDD): (918) 336-0700

Northwestern Okla. Independent Living Center 705 S. Oakwood Suite B-1
  Enid OK 73703 (Voice): (405) 237-8508 (TDD): 237-8508

Okla. Independent Living Resources Center 321 S. Third Suite 2
  McAlester OK 74501 (Voice): (918) 426-6220

Progressive Independence 121 N. Porter Norman OK 73071
  (Voice): (405) 321-3203 (TDD): 321-3203

Ability Resources 1724 East 8th St. Tulsa OK 74104
  (Voice): (918) 592-1235 (TDD): 592-1235

Oregon

Disabilities Advisory Coalition P.O. Box 10864 Eugene OR 97440
  (Voice): (503) 689-8675

Independent Abilities Center 290 NE C Street Grants Pass OR 97526
  (Voice/TDD): (503) 479-4275

SPOKES Unlimited P.O. Box 7896 Klamath Falls OR 97602
  (Voice): (503) 883-7547 (TDD): 883-7547

Access Oregon 2600 SE Belmont Suite A Portland OR 97214
  (Voice): (503) 230-1225 (TDD): 230-1225

Volunteer Braille Services 4001 N.E. Halsey Portland OR 97232
  (Voice): (503) 284-3339 (TDD): 284-3339

Pennsylvania

Lehigh Valley Center for Independent Living 1501 Lehigh Street
  Allentown PA 18103-3813 (Voice): (215) 791-7870 (TDD): 791-7875

Center for Independent Living of Southcentral PA 1501 - 11th Ave.
  Mezzanine Level Altoona PA 16601 (Voice/TDD): (814) 949-1905

Center for Independent Living of Central Pennsylvania 2331 Market St.
  Camp Hill PA 17011 (Voice): (717) 731-1900 (TDD): 731-1077

Erie Independence House 2222 Filmore Avenue Erie PA 16506-2943
  (Voice): (814) 838-7222 (TDD): 838-8115

Susquehanna Independent Living Center 1851 Charter Lane Lancaster PA 17605-0396 (Voice): (717) 397-2168 (TDD): 397-4193

North Central Center for Independent Living 1722 West Market Street Lewisburg PA 17837 (Voice): (717) 524-9695 (TDD): 524-9695

Resources for Living Independently One Winding Way Suite 108 Philadelphia PA 19131 (Voice): (215) 581-0666 (TDD): 581-0664

Three Rivers Center for Independent Living 7110 Penn Ave. Pittsburgh PA 15208 (Voice): (412) 371-7700 (TDD): 371-7700

Northeastern Pennsylvania Center for Independent Living 431 Wyoming Av. Lower Level Scranton PA 18503 (Voice/TDD): (717) 344-7211

Berks County Center for Independent Living 899 Penn Avenue Sinking Spring PA 19608 215 670-0734 (TDD): 670-0753

Tri-County Partnership for Independent Living 120 East Hallam Avenue Washington PA 15301-3404 (Voice/TDD): (412) 223-5115

Rhode Island

PARI Independent Living Center 500 Prospect St. Pawtucket RI 02860 (Voice): (401) 725-1966 (TDD): 725-1966

IN-SIGHT Independent Living 43 Jefferson Blvd. Warwick RI 02888 (Voice): (401) 941-3322

Ocean State Center for Independent Living 59 West Shore Road Warwick RI 02889(Voice): (401) 738-1013 (TDD): 738-1015

South Carolina

SC VR Independent Living Program 1410 Boston Ave. West Columbia SC 29171-0015 (Voice): (803) 822-5314

South Dakota

Opportunities for Independent Living P.O. Box 1571 Aberdeen SD 57402-1571 (Voice): (605) 622-2298

Western Resources for DisABLED Independence 36 E Chicago Rapid City SD 57701 (Voice): (605) 394-1930 (TDD): 394-1930

Communication Service for the Deaf 3520 Gateway Lane Sioux Falls SD 57106 (Voice): (605) 339-6718 (TDD): 339-6718

Prairie Freedom Center for Disabled 301 South Garfield Ave.
Sioux Falls SD 57104 (Voice): (605) 339-6558 (TDD): 339-6558

Tennessee

Memphis Center for Independent Living 163 North Angelus
Memphis TN 38104 (Voice): (901) 726-6404 (TDD): 726-6404

Tri State Resource & Advocacy for Ind. Living 1090 Chamberlain Ave.
Chattanooga, TN 37404 (Voice): (615) 622-2172

Texas

Panhandle Action Center for Independent Living 3608 S. Washington
Amarillo TX 79110 (Voice): (806) 352-1500 (TDD): 352-8630

Provence Center for Independent Living 600 New York Arlington TX
76010 (Voice): (817) 275-3369

Austin Resource Center for Independence 5555 North Lamar Suite J-125
Austin TX 78751 (Voice): (512) 467-0744 (TDD): 467-0744

Tri-County Awareness Association P.O. Box 875 Crockett TX 75835
(Voice): (409) 544-2811 (TDD): 544-7315

Dallas Center for Independent Living 8625 King George Dr. Dallas TX
75235 (Voice): (214) 631-6900 (TDD): 630-5411

Disabled Ability Resource Environment 8929 Viscount Suite 101 El Paso
TX 79925 (Voice): (915) 591-0800 (TDD): 591-0800

Reach Independent Living Center 617 Seventh Ave. Ft. Worth TX 76104
(Voice): (817) 870-9082 (TDD): 870-9086

Houston Center for Independent Living 7000 Regency Square Blvd.
Houston TX 77036 (Voice): (713) 974-4621 (TDD): 974-4621

Independent Life Styles P.O. Box 571874 Houston TX 77257
(Voice): (713) 784-5339

LIFE Independent Living Center 4514 Englewood Ave. Lubbock TX
79414-1227 (Voice): (806) 795-5433 (TDD): 795-5433

San Antonio Indep. Living Services 5101 San Pedro San Antonio TX
78212-1400 (Voice): (512) 734-9971 (TDD): 734-9971

Utah

OPTIONS for Independence 1095 N. Main Logan UT 84321
(Voice): (801) 753-5353 (TDD): 753-5353

Active Re-Entry 451 South Carbon Avenue Price UT 84501
(Voice): (801) 637-4950 (TDD): 637-4950

Utah Independent Living Center 764 South 200 West Salt Lake City UT
84101-2700 (Voice): (801) 359-2457 (TDD): 359-2457

Southern Utah Independent Living Center 206 North 1000 East St.
George UT 84770 (Voice): (801) 673-7579

Vermont

Vermont Association for the Blind 37 Elmwood Ave. Burlington VT
05401 (Voice): (802) 863-1358 (TDD): 863-1358

Vermont Center for Independent Living 174 River Street Montpelier VT
05602 (Voice): (802) 229-0501 (TDD): 229-0501

Virginia

Appalachian Independence Center 230 Charwood Drive Abingdon VA
24210 (Voice): (703) 628-2969 (TDD): 628-4931

Endependence Center of N. Virginia 2111 Wilson Blvd. Arlington VA
22201 (Voice): (703) 525-3268 (TDD): 525-3268

Independence Resource Center 201 West Main Street #8
Charlottesville VA 22901 (Voice): (804) 971-9629 (TDD): 971-9629

Woodrow Wilson Center for Independent Living Box W37
Fishersville VA 24401 (Voice): (703) 332-7103 (TDD): 332-7103

Peninsula Center for Independent Living 11832 Canon Blvd. Suite F
Newport News VA 23606 (Voice): (804) 873-0817 (TDD): 873-0817

Endependence Center Janaf Office Bldg. Suite 601 Norfolk VA 23502
(Voice): (804) 461-8007 (TDD): 461-7527

Central Virginia Independent Living Center 2900 West Broad St.
Richmond VA 23230-1049 (Voice): (804) 353-6503 (TDD): 353-6583

Center for Independence for the Disabled 1502-D Williamson Road NE
Roanoke VA 24012 (Voice): (703) 342-1231 (TDD): 342-1939

Shenandoah Valley Independent Living Center 21 South Kent Street
Winchester VA 22601 (Voice): (703) 662-4452 (TDD): 662-4452

Washington

Vision and Independent Living Services 2400 Queen Street
Bellingham WA 98226 (Voice): (206) 647-0309

Independent Lifestyle Services 306 North Main St. Ellensburg WA 98926
(Voice): (509) 962-9620

Everett Coalition People with Disabilities 1301 Hewett Everett WA
98201 (Voice): (206) 252-6456

Center for Independence 407 14th Ave. S.E. Puyallup WA 98372
(Voice): (206) 848-6661 (TDD): 848-6661

Community Service Center for the Deaf 2366 Eastlake Ave. East #312
Seattle WA 98122 (Voice): (206) 322-9446 (TDD): 322-9446

Community Services for the Blind 9709 Third Avenue NE #100
Seattle WA 98115 (Voice): (206) 525-5556 (TDD): 525-5556

Disabilities Law Project 1524 Queen Anne North Seattle WA 98109
(Voice): (206) 284-9733 (TDD): 284-9733

Independent Living Center Northwest 2600 South Walker Seattle WA
98144 (Voice): (206) 328-1403 (TDD): 328-1403

Washington Coalition of Citizens with disABILITIES 3530 Stone Way N.
Seattle WA 98103 (Voice): (206) 461-4550 (TDD): 461-4550

Coalition of Responsible Disabled North 908 Howard Suite 10
Spokane WA 99201 (Voice): (509) 326-6355 (TDD): 326-6355

Tacoma Area Coalition of Individuals with Disabilities 6315 S. 19th St.
Tacoma WA 98466-6217 (Voice/TDD): (206) 565-9000

Coalition of Handicapped Organizations P.O. Box 2129 Vancouver WA
98668-2129 (Voice): (206) 693-8819 (TDD): 693-8835

West Virginia

Mountain State Center for Independent Living 329 Prince Street
Beckley WV 25801 (Voice/TDD): (304) 255-0122

Appalachian Center for Independent Living 1023 Washington St. West
Charleston WV 25302-1441 (Voice/TDD): (304) 342-6328

Mountain State Center for Independent Living 914-1/2 Fifth Avenue
Huntington WV 25701 (Voice): (304) 525-3324 (TDD): 525-3324

NC West Virginia Center for Independent Living 1000 Elmer W. Prince
Drive Morgantown WV 26505 (Voice/TDD): (304) 599-3636

Wisconsin

Access to Independence 22 North Second Street Madison WI 53704
(Voice): (608) 251-7575 (TDD): 251-7731

Center for Independent Living University of Wisconsin-Stoutr
Menomonie WI 54751 (Voice): (715) 232-2150 (TDD): 232-2150

S.E. Wisconsin Center for Independence 6222 West Capitol Drive
Milwaukee WI 53216 (Voice): (414) 438-5622 (TDD): 438-5627

Society's Assets 1511 Washington Avenue Racine WI 53403
(Voice): (414) 637-9128 (TDD): 552-9656

North Country Independent Living P.O. Box 1245 Superior WI 54880
(Voice): (715) 392-9118 (TDD): 392-9118

Independent Living Services 1200 Lake View Dr. Wausau WI 54401
(Voice): (715) 848-4390 (TDD): 848-4390

Wyoming

Independent Living 246 S. Center Casper WY 82601
(Voice): (307) 266-6956 (TDD): 266-6956

Appendix C
Products and materials

General information on accommodations, auxiliary aids

Job Accommodation Network (800) 526-7234

ADA Technical Assistance Centers (see Appendix B)

Attitudes/sensitivity training materials and workshops

Workshops Milt Wright & Associates 19151 Parthenia St. Northridge CA 91324 (818) 349-0858

Videotapes "Nobody's Burning Wheelchairs" $35 15-minute videotape on working with people with disabilities and "Part of the Team" $15 18-minute videotape on disabled workers both available from National Easter Seal Society Administrative Services Dept. 70 E. Lake St. Chicago IL 60601 (800) 221-6827

"Better Communication between Hard of Hearing and Hearing People" $1.50 booklet available from Self Help for Hard of Hearing People 7800 Wisconsin Ave. Bethesda MD 20814 (301) 657-4112

"Getting Through" 22-minute audiotape simulates hearing loss to help you better understand hearing difficulties of hard of hearing people. $6.50 available from Self Help for Hard of Hearing People 7800 Wisconsin Ave. Bethesda MD 20814 (301) 657-4112

Signage, general (wheelchair access; TDD symbol, etc.)

General access and braille signs $10-$25 Best Manufacturing Company 1202 N. Park Ave., Montrose CO 81401-3170 (800) 235 2378

General access and braille signs $6 up also individual lettering and custom sign work Scott Plastics Co. Box 1047 Tallevast FL 34270 (800) 237-9447

Assistive listening systems

Publications: "Large Room Listening Systems for Hard of Hearing People" $4.90 **and** "Audio Induction Loops" $4.90 available from Self Help for Hard of Hearing People 7800 Wisconsin Ave. Bethesda MD 20814 (301) 657-4112

General information available from Self Help for Hard of Hearing People, Inc.'s Assistive Devices Demonstration Center Open 10-4 weekdays. 7800 Wisconsin Ave. Bethesda MD 20814 (301) 657-4112

Captioning (for videotapes)

Open or closed-captioning put onto videotape by The Caption Center WGBH Educational Foundation, Boston MA (617) 492-2777

Pamphlet: "What is Real-Time Captioning and How Can I use It?" $1.50 from: Self Help for Hard of Hearing People 7800 Wisconsin Ave. Bethesda MD 20814 (301) 657-4112

Sign language interpreters

Registry of Interpreters for the Deaf can provide a list of registered interpreters in your city or you may purchase a booklet of registered interpreters nationwide for $15 contact: Registry of Interpreters for the Deaf 8719 Colesville Rd., Suite 310 Silver Spring MD 20910 (301) 608 0050

Sign Language Associates has national referrals in other cities Silver Spring, MD (301) 588 7591

Telecommunications Devices for the Deaf (TDDs)

Available from: Krown Research (800) 833 4968
UltraTec (800) 233-9130
AT&T (800) 833-3232
PhoneTTY (201) 489-7889

Visual detection systems

Flashers, door knock signals, etc. available from Weitbrecht Communications Santa Monica, CA (Voice/TDD):(800) 233-9130

Braille/raised letter signs

Braille signs, various kinds $10-$25 available from Best Manufacturing Company 1202 N. Park Ave., Montrose CO 81401 (800) 235 2378

Braille signage, raised symbols for elevators also individual lettering; custom sign work $6 up Scott Plastics Co. Box 1047 Tallevast, FL 34270 (800) 237-9447

General information on computers, printing and technology for blind people

National Federation of the Blind (ask for the Technology Center) 1800 Johnson St. Baltimore MD 21230 (301) 659-9314

Enlargement of materials into large print for blind

(Local quick-print services can enlarge copy; see Chapter 6 for details)

Duplication of cassette audio tapes for blind people

(see your phone book for local audio or cassette tape duplication services)

Braille computer printers

The Braille Blazer Printer $1,699 Available from Blazie Engineering 3660 Mill Green Road, Street MD 21154 (301) 879 4944 prints on 8 1/2 by 11-inch braille fanfold paper, which they also sell

Romeo RB 20 Printer $2700 (somewhat faster than Braille Blazer) available from Enabling Technologies   Stewart, FL Sales: B. T Kimbrough (703) 683-5818 prints on 11 x 11 1/2 standard Braille paper

Braille printing paper

11 x 11 1/2 -inch standard computer braille paper, fanfold available from National Federation of the Blind (ask for the Technology Center) 1800 Johnson St. Baltimore MD 21230 (301) 659-9314 $39 for 1300 sheets

Braille wordprocessing conversion computer programs

Turbo Braille $249 converts standard IBM-compatible wordprocessing (WordPerfect, etc.) files into braille for printing

AutoBraille $195 memory resident print spooler program

Turbo Braille/AutoBraille package $395 Available from Kansys, Inc. 1016 Ohio St., Lawrence KS 66044 (800) 279 4880

Braille printing — small jobs/transcription services

Metrolina Association for the Blind 8 1/2 x 11-inch page $.30/page plus setup from (ask for: Mary Klattenhoff) 704 Louise Ave. Charlotte NC 28204 (704) 372-3870

Kansys, Inc. 1016 Ohio St., Lawrence KS 66044 (800) 279 4880

(or see local organizations of blind people in your phone directory)

Braille printing — large jobs (500-plus copies)

National Braille Press, Boston (617) 266-6160
American Printing House for the Blind, Louisville, KY (502) 895-2405
Braille Institute, Los Angeles (213) 663-1111
Associated Services for the Blind (215) 627-0600
Clovernook Opportunities for the Blind, Cincinatti (513) 522-3860

Physical access how-to

Two free pamphlets "The Americans with Disabilities Act: Removing Barriers in Places of Public Accommodation" "readily-achievable" things to do to remove barriers (with numerous photos of accessible solutions) and "Adapt To A Better Design," includes numerous photos Eastern Paralyzed Veterans Association 78-80 Astoria Blvd., Jackson Heights NY 11370 (718) 803-3782 (800) 444-0120 (in NY State)

Architectural consulting Barrier-Free Environments, Inc. Raleigh, NC (919) 782-7823

Index

ABOUT SOME OF THE PEOPLE IN THIS BOOK:

Frank Bowe, Ph.D. , a professor at Hofstra University, has worked on disability issues since the early 1970s. He is the author of *Handicapping America* and *Rehabilitating America.*

Diane Coleman is an attorney and community organizer for American Disabled for Attendant Programs Today.

Michael Collins is a member of the Washington State Governor's Committee on Disability Issues and Employment and the Region 10 Disability and Business Technical Assistance Center.

Richard Dodds is Project Director for the Region 2 Disability and Business Technical Assistance Center.

Sy Dubow is Director of the National Center for Law and the Deaf.

Stan Greenberg is Director of the Westside Center for Independent Living in Los Angeles.

Amy Hasbrouck is Director of Education and Advocacy at the Boston Center for Independent Living.

Howie the Harp is Director of the Oakland Independence Support Center.

Cass Irvin, a longtime disability rights activist, is President of Access to the Arts, Inc. in Louisville, Kentucky.

Geri Jewell, a comedian best known for her role as Blair's cousin Geri in Norman Lear's "The Facts Of Life," now works as a consultant with Milt Wright & Associates in Northridge, California.

Barbara Judy is Project Director for the Job Accommodation Network.

June Kailes, a consultant in private practice, provides training in management for disability organizations and in disability policy issues. She writes frequently about disability issues.

Bree Walker Lampley is a news anchor on KCBS-TV in Los Angeles.

Ruth Lusher is Director of the Office of Technical and Information Services of the U.S. Architectural and Transportation Barriers Compliance Board.

Ronald L. Mace, A.I. A. is President of Barrier Free Environments, an architectural firm.

Connie Martinez is an advisor with Capitol People First of Sacramento, California.

T. J. Monroe works as a self-advocate and consultant in Connecticut.

Bonnie O'Day is Director of the Boston Center for Independent Living.

Deborah Gately McKeen has been an organizer with the Cape Organization for Rights of the Disabled in Hyannis, Mass.

Marilynn J. Phillips, Ph.D., is a professor of at Morgan State University.

Dianne Piastro's weekly "Living With A Disability" column is distributed to over 300 newspapers nationwide.

Liz Savage is National Training Director for the Disability Rights Education & Defense Fund.

Gregory Solas, a former ironworker, is an activist in Rhode Island.

Lorelee Stewart, Director of the Independent Living Center of the North Shore in Lynn, Mass. , currently serves as Vice President of the National Council on Independent Living.

Jo Waldron is President of Phoenix Management, Inc., a management consulting firm, and a member of the President's Committee on Employment of Persons with Disabilities.

Steven Weiner is Director of the Careers Center at Gallaudet University.

Marian S. Vessels is Director of the Maryland Governor's Committee on Employment of People with Disabilities.

Patrisha Wright, Director of Governmental Affairs for the Disability Rights Education & Defense Fund, was a chief negotiator on the Americans with Disabilities Act.